*Henry James*

# Henry James

## The Writer and His Work

❧

Tony Tanner

The University of Massachusetts Press

Amherst, 1985

Copyright © 1985 by Tony Tanner
ALL RIGHTS RESERVED
Printed in the United States of America
Designed by Barbara Werden
Set in Linoterm Sabon at the University
of Massachusetts Press
Printed and bound by Cushing-Malloy, Inc.

The chapters in this book were published originally in the United Kingdom as
individual pamphlets in the series "Writers and
Their Work" by the British Council, 1979–1981.

LIBRARY OF CONGRESS CATALOGING IN PUBLICATION DATA

Tanner, Tony.
Henry James: the writer and his work.

"Published originally . . . as individual pamphlets in
the series 'Writers and their work' by the British
Council, 1979–1981"—Verso t.p.
Bibliography: p.
Includes index.
1. James, Henry, 1843–1916—Criticism and
interpretation.   I. Title.
PS2124.T34   1985     813'.4     85–1168
ISBN 0–87023–492–7

*Frontispiece*
Portrait of Henry James by K. McClellan.
Courtesy of The College Archives, Smith College,
Northampton, Massachusetts.

*To*

*John Barrell*

*and*

*Christopher Prendergast*

# Contents

# Preface

SOME YEARS AGO I was asked by the British Council to write three pamphlets on Henry James. The intention of these pamphlets (called "Writers and Their Work") is to provide an introduction to a particular writer, stressing the works but also relating them, necessarily rather sketchily, to the biographical facts of his or her life. With the guidance of Ian Scott-Kilvert of the British Council (whose help I am happy to have a chance to acknowledge here) I wrote the pamphlets and now (with the encouragement of Bruce Wilcox of the University of Massachusetts Press, for which I am most grateful) I am offering these pamphlets, somewhat amended, as a small book. Like the pamphlets, it is not aimed at the reader already familiar with the works and life of James; by the same token it is not intended to supply utterly basic information and plot summaries for some notionally completely ignorant reader. The hope is, rather, that it may interest and even stimulate any educated reader who has read some James but is in no way a specialist and who might care to have a short account of the development of his complete works with some biographical background. In a way it is a short biography of James's imagination in its seemingly inexhaustible inventiveness and continuously amazing productivity. It does not hope or attempt to supplant or supersede the late F. W. Dupee's book on Henry James which became an essential introduction to the man and his work some thirty-five years ago. But every age needs to be reintroduced to—or to reintroduce itself to—a major writer and it is that need I am addressing in offering a brief reintroduction to Henry James for our times. For the Henry James specialist it will have little or no interest, and when it comes to biographical material I have, of course, nothing to add to the magnificent work of Leon Edel. In attempting to point to interesting and even crucial aspects of James's eighteen finished novels as well as trying to give some sense of his other writings, all in a book shorter than many of James's novellas, I necessarily have been forced to an extreme of compression. My hope is that there may be at least one compensating advantage, namely a conveyed sense of the unique imagination and intelligence of James as he explored, developed, defined, discovered and rediscovered, and expressed himself throughout all his work. It is that lifelong undertaking, adventure, and enterprise—the parabola of James's ever self-renewing creativity—that I have tried to describe as a single story. It need hardly be stressed what abbreviations, foreshortenings, and omissions such an undertaking entails. I can only hope that the story as I have told it will be of some interest to those who, perhaps, know one or two installments of it and would like to know some more. In James's *The Bostonians*, Olive Chancellor cries out at one point: "A voice, a human voice, is what we want." It is a perennial need and in that particular novel it is arguable that, truly speaking, there is finally no "human voice" to be heard. Except for the sympathizing, supervising voice of the author. Arguably, too, it is mainly our great writers who can remind us what a truly "human voice" can be. And that is another way of saying what I have attempted to do in this book: to listen to James's "voice" as it articulates itself throughout his life's work and to try to transcribe and define some of its rare "human-ness" and irreplaceable, unmistakable, singularity. Such an attempt is doomed to abrupt inadequacy and simplifying approximations. But it seemed an attempt worth making given the intention of the series for which it was initially written. If our civilization still has any kind of a "human voice" then Henry James is indisputably part of it.

After twenty-five years of reading James and works on James it would be idle and impossible for me to attempt to single out specific debts (though I do want to thank Warner Berthoff for some very helpful comments on the pamphlets before I assembled them as this book). This book itself comes out of—is part of—the chorus of voices that James himself engendered. The dedication itself is simply intended as a gesture of respect and gratitude to two indispensable friends and colleagues.

*February 1985*                              TONY TANNER
                                             King's College
                                             Cambridge

*Henry James*

# I

## America and Europe, 1843–1881:

## "A Complex Fate"

N 1882, the authoritative and esteemed American critic William Dean Howells wrote an article on Henry James, Jr., in *Century Magazine* that helped to precipitate, or rather exacerbate, a controversy, not only about the respective virtues of English and American writing, but about the very nature and future of fiction itself, as well. He praised Henry James in the following terms:

> His race is Irish on his father's side and Scotch on his mother's, to which mingled strains the generalizer may attribute, if he likes, that union of vivid expression and dispassionate analysis which has characterized his work from the first. . . . If we take him at all we must take him on his own ground, for clearly he will not come to ours. . . . We must agree, then, to take what seems a fragment instead of a whole, and to find, when we can, a name for this new kind of fiction. Evidently it is the character, not the fate, of his people which occupies him; when he has fully developed their character, he leaves them to what destiny the reader pleases.
>
> The analytic tendency seems to have increased with him as his work has gone on. . . . No other novelist, except George Eliot, has dealt so largely in analysis of motive, has so fully explained and commented upon the springs of action in the per-

sons of the drama, both before and after the facts. These novelists are more alike than any others in their processes, but with George Eliot an ethical purpose is dominant, and with Mr. James an artistic purpose. . . . The art of fiction has, in fact, become a finer art in our day than it was with Dickens and Thackeray. We could not suffer the confidential attitude of the latter now, nor the mannerism of the former. . . . The new school derives from Hawthorne and George Eliot rather than any others; but it studies human nature much more in its wonted aspects, and finds its ethical and dramatic examples in the operation of lighter but not really less vital motives. The moving accident is certainly not its trade; and it prefers to avoid all manner of dire catastrophes. It is largely influenced by French fiction in form. . . . This school, which is so largely of the future as well as the present, finds its chief exemplar in Mr. James; it is he who is shaping and directing American fiction, at least. . . . Will the reader be content to accept a novel which is an analytic study rather than a story, which is apt to leave him arbiter of the destiny of the author's creations? . . . A novelist he is not, after the old fashion, or after any fashion but his own; yet since he has finally made his public in his own way of storytelling—or call it character-painting if you prefer—it must be conceded that he has chosen best for himself and his readers in choosing the form of fiction for what he has to say. It is, after all, what a writer has to say rather than what he has to tell that we care for nowadays. In one manner or other the stories were all told long ago; and now we want merely to know what the novelist thinks about persons and situations. Mr. James gratifies this philosophic desire. . . . I own that I like a finished story; but then I also like those which Mr. James seems not to finish. This is probably the position of most of his readers, who cannot very logically account for either preference. We can only be sure that we have here an analist (*sic*), or analyst, as we choose, who fascinates us from his first page to his last, whose narrative or whose comment may enter into any minuteness of detail without fatiguing us, and can only truly grieve us when it ceases.

Something of the background to these remarks—which caused much offense, anger, and attempted rebuttal—should be sketched in if we are to understand and appreciate in what ways Henry James was the "chief exemplar" of a new school of fiction, the future of which (not only in America) he was to be so instrumental in "shaping and directing." To quote a friend of Howells's, George Pelles, writing in 1888, "For a long time a wordy war has raged in the magazines and the newspapers between so-called realists and romanticists. . . . The ground is strewn with dead and dying reputations." It is this "war" we should say a word about, to comprehend something of what Henry James was trying to do in and with the novel, which seemed so new—and even incomprehensible—at the time.

The terms of the controversy were crude, and a word like "realism" now begs more questions for us than it answers. But the opposition seemed clear enough then. The great majority of readers wanted novels that, to put it tersely, were either sentimental or sensational. The popular novels were "dramatic" and "romantic"; they concentrated on externalities of action and deployed stereotypical characters and emotions. In a debased use of the term, these novels were thought to be "idealistic," inasmuch as they showed ideal characters experiencing ideal emotions. Anything written under the name of "realism" was thought to be a threat to this "idealism." What this popular novel distinctly avoided was "psychological" analysis, which was "scientific," anti-idealistic, heartless. In the majority of contemporary reviews, the very word "analysis" was invariably used in a pejorative sense. So James's novels would be castigated for offering "what may be stigmatized as super-subtle analyses, ultra-refined phrases, fine-spun nothings" (Annie R. M. Logan, *Current Literature,* 3 December 1904). Or again, William Morton Payne, reviewing *The Bostonians,* complained that the author had been "wearisomely minute in his . . . analysis," cluttering the story with a "mass of analysis of trifling things."

WE MAY NOTE the tacit but prevailing assumption that "story" and "analysis" were antipathetic, if not mutually exclusive phenomena, the latter working to the detriment of the former. Indeed, James's novels and stories were often referred to as "studies" rather than novels, almost as we might think of Freud's case histories as being necessarily different from any kind of novel, although were it not for their factual basis we might readily regard them as a species of psychoanalytic fiction. But during the years of James's early career, there was little idea that the "analysis" might itself *be* the "story." Indeed, there was downright hostility to the presence of "analysis" in fictional narrative. To quote Henry Nash Smith:

> The new novel took itself seriously and demanded that its readers do the same. It refused to offer itself as merely an amusement or as a sentimental debauch. Instead, just as Margaret Oliphant has castigated Hawthorne in the 1850s, reviewers complained again and again that James insisted on introducing them to the dissecting room of the anatomist, with repulsive associations of blood and stench and callousness. When "dissection" becomes "vivisection," the notion of callousness acquires overtones of sadism. (*Democracy and the Novel* [Oxford University Press, 1978], p. 145)

As Smith points out, there was a lot of implicit populist antiintellectualism in these early reviews of James, and oft repeated charges of "interminable analysis" and heartless "vivisection" barely concealed a deep disinclination to inquire too curiously, or inquire at all, into the complex workings of the human mind and the highly problematical moral issues that were posed by such deep probings. As an anonymous reviewer wrote in 1900 (in *Outlook*), James's stories are "too subtle, too psychological, too analytical, for the purposes of fiction." I have stressed this early resistance to James's work at some length because we have come to think of him mainly as "the Master," admired and deeply respected by a whole range of major twentieth-century writers. It is important to realize what he had to struggle *against* as he gradually developed a new kind of fiction that played a major part in what Smith calls "the liquidation of nineteenth-century culture," and served to effect radical changes in the conception of what a novel could be and do.

## II

Henry James was born in New York City in 1843, an urban beginning that from the start left him relatively untouched by the dominant American influences which were represented by the

Transcendentalist writers of New England (best represented by Emerson and Thoreau). His whole "education" and upbringing were calculated to give him a multiple and international perspective on various cultures, and ensured that he would not, or could not, be contained within the orthodoxies of any one school of thought or theory of fiction, American, English, or European. His father, himself a remarkable and independent figure, had rejected the Calvinism of his father (an Irish immigrant), and was influenced mainly by the philosophy of Swedenborg, traces of whose thought have been detected in his son's work. Henry James Senior gave his children an unusually free rein during their childhood, which doubtless contributed to the notable "freedom" of their thought. Henry's brother William was to become a major American philosopher and psychologist, whose ideas about the "stream of consciousness" can be related to the fictional practice of his brother. Henry was taken abroad when he was six months old, and his earliest impressions and memories were of Europe (one of his earliest memories was of the Napoleonic column in the Place Vendôme). He returned to Albany and New York when he was nearly three and spent his boyhood in a number of private schools in New York, and by the age of twelve was well steeped in the atmosphere of Manhattan. Then in 1855 his father took his family abroad and for three years the children had a number of tutors and governesses in Geneva, London, and Paris. What kind of formal education Henry absorbed during these years would be hard to estimate, but he not only became an avid reader of the fiction of France and England, as well as of America, he also acquired a sense of the value of individual freedom and a habit of detachment from any kind of group commitment. He lived among, and off, literature, museums, galleries, and the variegated impressions of the changing cultural scenes through which he passed.

In 1858 the family returned to America; then a year later Henry went to Geneva. He returned and the family settled in Newport, Rhode Island. During this period he sustained a strange back injury (while helping to put out a fire) about which there has been much speculation, since, among other things, it prevented him from taking any active part in the Civil War. In 1862 he entered Harvard Law School, but soon withdrew; he had already started

writing articles and short stories, and he realized that he was
not cut out for any of the orthodox professions. He was to stay
in America until 1870 when he made his first adult journey to
England (where he met Rossetti, William Morris, and Ruskin),
France, and Italy, and it was in that year that he published his first
novel, *Watch and Ward*, written in Boston. Between 1872 and
1874 he was again in Europe, particularly Rome, and it was there
he began *Roderick Hudson*. Again he returned to America, where
he attempted to make a living from literary journalism in New
York. *Roderick Hudson* was published in 1875, as were a number
of important short stories and a book of travel sketches. From
1875–76 he was back in Paris (where he met such eminent writers
as Turgenev, Flaubert, Zola, de Goncourt, Daudet, and Maupas-
sant). It was there he wrote *The American*.

This year seems to have been decisive, for in December 1876 he
decided to settle in London, which was to remain his base, if not
his "home," for the rest of his life. During these years, James had
learned a great deal about the "art of fiction" from English and
European writers—one might single out Balzac, Turgenev, and
George Eliot—but it is worth remembering that he was still an
American, albeit a very unusual and unanchored one, with a
unique multinational tone. A passage from a letter to Thomas
Sergeant Perry written in 1867 is worth keeping in mind.

We are Americans born—*il faut en prendre son parti*. I look
upon it as a great blessing; and I think that to be an American is
an excellent preparation for culture. We have exquisite qualities as a race, and it seems to me that we are ahead of the European races in the fact that more than either of them we can deal
freely with forms of civilization not our own, can pick and
choose and assimilate and in short (aesthetically, etc.) claim
our property where we find it. To have no national stamp has
hitherto been a regret and a drawback, but I think it not unlikely that American writers may yet indicate that a vast intellectual fusion and synthesis of the various National tendencies of
the world is the condition of more important achievements
than any we have seen. We must of course have something of
our own—something distinctive and homogeneous—and I
take it that we shall find it in our moral consciousness, our un-
precedented spiritual lightness and vigour.

8

These are sentiments that would be echoed by subsequent American expatriate writers, such as Ezra Pound and T. S. Eliot, who were to be instrumental in shaping a new kind of modern poetry. They are not the words of an "outsider" as we have come to understand that word, but rather of a supranationalist, a would-be synthesist of the best achievements of various cultural forms, a citizen primarily of literature itself, his real domain the endless empire of the word.

Given his upbringing and the multiple cultural perspectives it afforded him, it is hardly surprising that Henry James should have developed what came to be known as the "international theme," often introducing the fine "moral consciousness" of the American into the rich cultural atmosphere of Europe, thus dramatizing the confrontation of different schemes of values, showing the "provincialism" of the American groping its way through the European social landscape, dense with moral ambiguities, saturated in history, and dominated by old precedents, manners, and sophistications. But we would be making a mistake to see his work as simply contrasting American "innocence" with European "experience." As he said of himself, it was a "complex fate" to be an American living in Europe, and his sense of that complexity carried over into his fiction, so there is never (or seldom) any melodramatic sense of American goodness succumbing to European intrigue, deviousness, and evil. Indeed, some of his morally culpable and evil intriguers are expatriate Americans, as we can see in *The Portrait of a Lady* (1881), a novel rightly reckoned in my opinion to mark his greatest achievement during what might be termed the first phase of his fictional writing, a period in which he was still to some extent trying to synthesize all he had learnt from the existing fiction of three cultures, as well as developing the style that was becoming distinctively his own.

### III

It is worth taking note of a few of James's very early short stories before moving on to a consideration of the novels. From the start, love appears as potentially lethal—as in his very first, rather crude story ("A Tragedy of Error"), in which a woman plans to murder her lame and unloved husband. James would scarcely be so crude again—the plottings and "killings" became much more subtle and devious. A subtler story concerns a young man recuperating in comfort and ease from Civil War wounds who suddenly takes a turn for the worse when he is possessed by a love for a young healthy woman who can only offer him dutiful affection. As is not uncommon in James, the passions are muffled but intense, explosive but unseen. Very little disturbs the elegant composure of the house, yet the man dies of "hopes deferred and shattered visions" after an evening of hectic social fulfillment. His death is considered "a most extraordinary case" (which is also the title of the story). Other stories concentrate on failures of communication, glimpsed unfulfilled possibilities of liaison, separations, and withdrawals. An afternoon walk brings two strangers to the very edge of passion, but somehow emotion is quietly strangled and a decorous departure supervenes. "Poor Richard" reveals how three men and a woman contrive to secure unhappiness for each other by death, deceit, or simply the ungrasped moment of opportunity: "They had come within an ace of a mutual understanding, and when a single movement of the hand of either would have jerked aside the curtain that hung between them, some malignant influence had paralysed them both." Another story inaugurates the theme of the disquieting discrepancy between social appearances and hidden personal realities, using what was to become a typical Jamesian device (also used by Hawthorne), the revealing portrait. A man is engaged to be married to a woman he considers to be the sum of all sweetness and virtue. Her portrait is painted by an artist who is also an old lover, and the husband-to-be is shocked by what he sees revealed in the picture—a lack of heart, of faith, of conscience: "What else was the meaning of that horrible blankness and deadness that quenched the light in her eyes and stole away the smile from her lips?" ("The Story of a Masterpiece").

There are stories that are mainly pegs on which to hang his accumulated clusters of impressions of Europe, gathered and hoarded by his "sympathetic retina" and habit of "trembling observation" (though one, "Travelling Companions," with its Venetian scenes, its young American heroine with "the divine gift of feeling" and her rich affectionate father, carries tiny adumbrations of his last major novels). One of these stories, "A Passionate Pilgrim," about an American visitor to Europe, in this case England, is, however, of particular importance, showing James probing well beyond "travelogue" as he examines in close detail the effects of a tradition-saturated England on a highly impressionable young American who comes to visit the home of his ancestors. The narrator starts by referring to England as a place "of which I had dreamed much but as yet knew nothing." The struggle between anticipatory dream and unavoidable, often contradictory knowledge—and the shock that can ensue—was often to be examined and dramatized by James. This narrator befriends the actual "passionate pilgrim," named Searle, who thinks he has some "valid claim" to a part of a country house and estate in Herefordshire. Legally the claim is perhaps doubtful, but metaphorically it is appropriate enough as he "comes into his own," as it were, when he visits the place. But the effects of all the wondrous impressions of old England are far from unambiguous, and if they are enriching they are fatally so. "His observation I soon perceived to be extremely acute. His almost passionate relish for the old, the artificial, and social, well-nigh extinct from its long inanition, began now to tremble and thrill with a tardy vitality. I watched in silent wonderment his strange metaphysical renascence." Once inside the house, and after meeting with differing receptions from his "relatives," Searle says to the narrator: " 'I'm not frightened, but I'm—O, EXCITED! This is life! This is living! My nerves—my heart—my brain! They are throbbing with the wildness of a myriad lives! . . . I shall tremble away into waves— waves—waves, and know the universe and approach my Maker.' " Searle is clearly very sick: "I may say that from this time forward, with my unhappy friend, I found it hard to distinguish between the play of fancy and the labor of thought, and to fix the balance between perception and illusion" (a problem that will occur in much of James's fiction in which perception and illusion feed into each other in the most problematical ways); later the narrator notes: "He was becoming more and more a disembodied observer and critic; the shell of sense, growing daily thinner and more transparent, transmitted the tremor of his quickened spirit."

Searle dies just when it seems he might come into his "inheritance." But James has noted many ambivalences in the situation and its outcome. The effect of England on a susceptible but starved sensibility could be disastrous, as the excess of "impressions" threatens to drown and dissolve the mental coherence of the American visitor (" 'I shall tremble away into waves' "), as he responds *too* intensely to the long-anticipated scenes of England, to the point at which his sanity is threatened. In addition—and this will become an important problem for James—as a person becomes more and more an "observer" (in itself an ambivalent role in James, as in Hawthorne and other novelists), what happens to "the body," or, more generally, the capacity for physical participation in life? The "disembodied observer," here feverishly alert and perceptive while corporeally dying, becomes a problematical figure for James, who was himself, after all, most supremely an "observer and critic."

But perhaps most interesting are the stories that concern themselves with the terrible silent rapacity of civilized people, the concealed jostlings for emotional power that take place with furtive intensity just below the social surface. See, for example, "A Light Man" in which the ruthless competitive egotism of two different men—both trying to ingratiate themselves with a foolish, rich old man in order to become his heir—masquerades on the one hand as exquisite, entertaining social manners, and on the other as a pious pseudoreligious dedication: in this instance, both of them lose. In "De Grey: A Romance," James uses a Hawthornesque family curse for its psychological possibilities, touching on the idea that, later, he would explore more deeply, that in any relationship one partner battens on to and drains the life energy of the other. Thus, all the women ever loved by the De Grey family have died young. The heroine, in love with the young De Grey, rejects the curse and goes ahead with her love affair—and this time, the man withers: "As she bloomed and prospered, he drooped and languished. While she was living for him, he was dying for her." What is here streaked with Gothic melodrama is later to become a subtler and arguably more frightening aspect of James's vision of human relationships. For we perhaps too often forget—charmed by his civilized tone—that for James there was beauty *and* terror in "conditions so highly organised," i.e., in civilized society. "Our imagination is always too timid" says one of his wiser characters. We prefer not to envisage the possibility of hidden atrocity under the smooth social surface, but for James it was a perpetual possibility—one for which he developed his art, in order to explore it more fully.

*Watch and Ward* was Henry James's first novel, written in 1870, and serialized in the following year in the *Atlantic Monthly* (not appearing in book form until 1878, by which time it had been heavily revised). It is often ignored, as James himself disregarded it when he came to assemble a collected edition of his work, yet he had high hopes for it when he wrote it (it was to be that elusive entity "The Great American Novel"!) and it is worth glancing briefly at the theme and arrangement of the novel, as it contains, albeit embryonically, seeds of some of his future work. A young to middle-aged man, Roger Lawrence, who is not notably active, attractive, or passionate and who has failed in his one attempt at a love affair, "adopts" a young girl, Nora Lambert, who is orphaned (in a rather melodramatic way—her father shoots himself in the hotel at which Lawrence is staying; one of the few actual pistol shots in James's fiction!). His motives for this "kindly" act of adoption are complex, overdetermined as we say after Freud. There is pity and there is generosity (though James was well aware of the concealed predatory nature of much of what passes for generosity); on the other hand, he is consciously conducting an "experiment," determined to bring Nora up as a perfect wife who will feel so "indebted" to him that she will choose to marry him—thus his act of kindness is not disinterested, because it is also a form of "investment" on which he expects to collect a return. Such treatment of another person, as part of an experiment, or as a form of investment, is always highly ambiguous in James. Lawrence has a "strenuous desire to fathom the depths of matrimony. He had dreamed of this gentle bondage as other men dream of the free unhoused condition of celibacy," so he chooses to "use" the initially rather plain and not very bright Nora to satisfy this dream. He sees himself as "a protector, a father, a brother" and he aspires to allow Nora all the freedom she needs to develop in her own way. As he "cunningly devised her happiness" he feels that "his small stale merits became fragrant with the virtue of unselfish use." At times, he thinks of Nora "as a kind of superior doll, a thing wound up with a key" (and there is much play with the idea of "keys" in the book, not only keys that unlock the heart, but also unconscious "sexual" ones, as in one famous scene in which Nora tries to find a "key" that is the right size to wind up her watch).

But the doll becomes very much alive and independent—" 'I am no one's child,' " she exclaims at one point, and as she starts to grow in beauty and intelligence, she threatens to shatter his "scheme" of "fashioning of a wife to order," and strike out on her own. She is attracted to two different men—Roger's cousin, Hubert, a plausible rhetorician, who "plays" at love as he plays at everything else, including theology (he is a clergyman, of a very worldly sort): and her so-called cousin, George Fenton, a rough virile man from the West, whose apparent masculinity and un-mannered strength initially attract Nora as representing every-thing that Roger, as a man, is not. When Nora discovers what Roger has been doing, she is appalled: "she must throw off these suffocating bounties which had been meant to bribe her to the service in which she had so miserably failed." She leaves his house, and experiences that crucial Jamesian sense of "freedom." "A day's freedom had come at last; a lifetime's freedom confronted her." But the "freedom" turns out to be very ambiguous, and when she turns to Hubert and Fenton for help, they both fail her in different ways. Fenton simply wants to make money out of re-turning her to Roger, while Hubert reveals his basic heartless egoism: "the central pivot of his being continued to operate with the most noiseless precision and regularity—the slim, erect, in-flexible *Ego*."

This is often the plight of the young woman seeking to be "free" in the world at large. She finds herself at the mercy of plau-sible but exploitative egoists who have no real concern for her as a unique and precious "other," but simply seek to use her for their own ends (this is to be one of the main themes of *A Portrait of a Lady*). Paradoxically, all Roger's planning and scheming for her was mainly to allow her to be free to be herself and develop her own potential to the uttermost—though, to be sure, the plan in-cludes a hope that in that freedom she will choose Roger as her husband (as she finally does). After her defection, he is ravaged by illness and prepares himself to accept a life of renunciation (another key theme in James), but Nora, after her experience of other men and the harsh heartlessness of the world at large, feels that she has come to perceive a secret truth. "Yes, she was in the secret of the universe, and the secret of the universe was that

Roger was the only man in it who had a heart." For this to happen, Roger has to cease to regard himself as her guardian, which imposed on her "the terrible burden of gratitude," and she has to forget her wardship and the sense that she is acting as his debtor, and choose him freely, and she finally does. Such happy resolutions are not common in James, but his sense of the infinite complexities in the relations between the sexes—so that "love" never comes clear and easy and uncomplicated—not only permeates this book, but would be present throughout his work, which is to be full of "watchers" and "warders," egoists and experimenters, exploiters and appropriators, the heartless always threatening to outdevise and displace those rarer few who do still "have a heart." And the figure of the loyal and devoted sufferer, made invalid by attempting to live in a world of ruthless competing egoisms, is one that will reappear in some of his major works. This mainly forgotten first novel in fact contains in embryo a lot of the themes, and some of the methods—the half-revealing, half-concealing conversation; the detailed summary of shifting states of consciousness and interior emotional ratiocination—that, in more complex forms, will be encountered in his subsequent work.

## V

*Roderick Hudson* was started in Europe in 1874 and was to be the first of many works in which James explored the problem of what it was to be an artist in his own time, problems of material and audience: *What* was he producing exactly, and *for whom* was he producing it? What was the morality of the artist, and what was his relation to the artistic wealth of the past? A short story written at this time, "The Madonna of the Future," carries an austere warning. An American artist in Italy plans to paint an immortal madonna, and speaks much of it. But when his friend finally sees the canvas, "I can hardly say that I was surprised at what I found—a canvas that was a mere dead blank, cracked and discolored by time. This was his immortal work." It turns out that he is better at making cynical, satirical little models of cats and monkeys—a kind of vengeful anti-idealism to make up for that vacant canvas. He dies shortly after his secret is out. The dangers of trying to make a contemporary work compete with the august masterpieces of other ages are clearly marked out. Where Hawthorne was visibly nervous about introducing his American artists into a Europe in which it was difficult to tell the richness from the rottenness (see *The Marble Faun*), Henry James found in the situation the perfect theme for his first exploration of the problems of the American artist. *Roderick Hudson* traces the short career of an American artist who opens himself up fully, indeed greedily, to European experience, with fatal results. Indeed, so short is the time between Hudson's first eager impressions of Rome and his fall, which must be considered a suicide, in the Swiss Alps, that James felt he had to apologize for the implausible rapidity of his deterioration. In the preface added later (for the 1910 collected edition of his works), James says that Hudson's "disintegration" occurs too quickly: "at the rate at which he falls to pieces, he seems to place himself beyond our understanding and sympathy." Aesthetically, the point is debatable. But the picture of an American artist rather quickly falling to pieces after an initial burst of great creative power is perhaps more appropriate than James realizes. It was Scott Fitzgerald who said that the lives of American writers contained no second acts. The remark hardly applies to James, but there is something almost prophetic in his picture of an American artist moving at such a pace that he would have no energy left after the crowded first act of his artistic life.

From the beginning when he is seen as a discontented student of law in a provincial American town, Hudson is seen as doing "everything too fast," and he characterizes himself as being driven by a "demon of unrest." Upon seeing one of Hudson's statues, Rowland Mallett, a rich friend who appreciates art but cannot produce any himself, offers to take Hudson to Europe and become his patron. Mallett is one of James's observers, and it is worth noting that James made, thus early, a clear distinction between the artist and the observer. ("My subject all blissfully, in face of difficulties, had defined itself . . . as not directly, in the least, my young sculptor's adventure. This it had been but indirectly, being all the while in essence and in final effect another man's, his friend's and patron's, view and experience of him. . . . The centre of interest throughout *Roderick Hudson* is in Rowland Mallett's consciousness, and the drama is the very drama of that consciousness." Thus James defines, retrospectively, what was to become a crucial subject for him—the drama of consciousness of the observer.) Roderick is depicted as having genius, "the sacred fire," and it takes him into regions well outside the boundaries of the social law of which he was so imperfect a student. Rowland Mallett has no genius and so, while capable of appreciating art and Italy, he can remain safely within the moral law. There is no doubt that James felt that genius could take a person into dangerous areas in which all conscience might be lost. As Mallett comes to realize, although genius is divine, it can be "capricious, sinister, cruel"; and he comes to think of Roderick as a fairly ruthless egotist. His worry about Roderick is that "the values in such a spirit" might not be "much larger than the voids," and, in the event, in this book the voids swallow up the values. The inflamed genius who set out from America ends his life as a hollow husk, burnt out, eclipsed, in a catatonic stupor. His fall from the mountain only completes the process of dying that has completely overtaken his inner life.

To illuminate some aspects of Roderick's doomed career it is helpful to notice the changing subjects of his sculpture. His first piece seen by Rowland is of a youth standing naked, drinking deeply from a gourd, and it is called "Thirst." Rowland asks if the drinker represents an "idea" or is a "pointed symbol," and Hudson agrees that his work represents innocence, youth, curiosity, drinking deeply of knowledge, pleasure, and experience. The one thing that Roderick does not mention as being represented by his symbolic work is any actual drink, such as wine. Yet when he gets to Europe he soon discovers the pleasures of real champagne as well as the inspiration of high ideals. Indeed, his downfall might be ascribed to a mixture of intoxications in which it becomes impossible for him to separate the ideal from the actual. Roderick's first successes as a sculptor in Italy are his monumental Adam and Eve—appropriate enough for an American artist. He speaks of going on to do David and "a ripping Christ" who will be "the perfection of form . . . to symbolise the perfection of spirit." In these early days his talk is always about ideas or ideal forms, including a prospective "magnificent image of my native land." It is at this time that Rowland first sees the problematical lady, Christina Light, who is, for him, "a glimpse of ideal beauty." If such beauty is wrong, he says, then he is happy to see her as the "incarnation of evil." Christina, although nominally American, has been brought up in Europe and is a deeply disturbing ambiguous female (James was to employ her again, in *The Princess*

*Casamassima*). She is a mixture of passions although she presents a totally indifferent face to the world; she may be the epitome of corruption, as she herself says, or the finest bloom of a fusion of cultures; she is capable of unpredictable metamorphoses. Roderick is intoxicated by her, while Rowland Mallett thinks her unsafe: "she was a complex, wilful, passionate creature who might easily draw down a too confident spirit into some strange underworld of unworthy sacrifices, not unfurnished with traces of others lost." Roderick's idealizing aspirations are discussed in terms of flight and gained altitudes of spirit, but once he has been intoxicated by the sight of Christina, his movement is irreversibly downwards. Rowland sees this happening and has a "vision of the wondrous youth, graceful and beautiful as he passed, plunging like a diver into a misty gulf. The gulf was destruction, annihilation, death. . . ."

After getting to know Christina, Roderick's art changes. He does a sculpture of a woman leaning back in a languid pose. Rowland, still the good New Englander, asks: "What does it mean?" Roderick, for the first time, disdains the notion of some extra dimension of ideal meaning. "Anything you please," he says. "A 'Lady conversing affably with a Gentleman.' " It is a totally secular piece, opaque to higher meanings, and, not surprisingly, Rowland is not sure that he likes it. Roderick's bust of Christina Light has more depth, but it reminds another artist, the perceptive Gloriani, of Salome. Roderick's art is now penetrating the mystery of the dangerous and destructive female. He has begun to dive.

At this point, a pompous American named Mr. Leavenworth comes to him and asks him to do a representation of Intellectual Refinement. To be fair, the younger Roderick would have found nothing ridiculous in so abstract a commission, but Mr. Leavenworth becomes for him a stifling and tedious presence chattering on about "spiritual art." One of Roderick's next pieces is of "a *lazzarone* [i.e., one of the lowest class of beggars in Naples] lounging in the sun." Mr. Leavenworth happens to come in and asks if it is something in the style of the "Dying Gladiator." " 'Oh no,' said Roderick seriously, 'he's not dying, he's only drunk.' " The righteous Mr. Leavenworth reproves him: "Ah, but intoxication, you know . . . is not a proper subject for sculpture. Sculpture shouldn't deal with transitory attitudes." Roderick has the better of the exchange, but a potentially serious point is being made. In a way, Roderick has turned attention from the eternal to the transitory, and the difference in his statues between the upstanding unfallen Adam and the prone drunken figure does offer an analogue for his own artistic life. Gloriani more than once speaks of Roderick coming down to earth, and in truth Roderick is more and more often seen lying down. More seriously, he is now intoxicated with the things of this world. His eye is no longer on Platonic ideas or eternal types; it is turned earthwards, into the bedeviling compounds of ordinary life. It is perhaps this that enables him to do such a touching and truthful bust of his mother for what is his last mentioned work. Not Adam and Eve, our biblical or mythical parents, but his actual individual parent—this again indicates the change that has come over Roderick's art.

In his feeling of adoration for Christina, Roderick goes beyond socially recognized good and evil; when she withdraws from him he cannot return to a form of life governed by those categories. He can only collapse into apathy and die. One general point made about Roderick summarizes something important about the American artist. As Rowland sees Roderick, "the great and characteristic point with him was the perfect separateness of his sensibility. He never saw himself as part of a whole; only as the clear-cut, sharp-edged, isolated individual, rejoicing or raging, as the case might be, but needing in each case to affirm himself." A perfectly separate sensibility is one that cannot truly be socialized: the affirmation of the artist is inseparable from his isolation, perhaps finally from his destruction—these are two propositions that James's novel may fairly be said to bear out. The difficulty for the artist to see himself as "part of a whole" is not restricted to Americans, but it seems to have remained for American artists a more constant problem. It is relevant to note that a perfect separate self is unlikely to be in harmony with the democratic en masse. And, in its way, this was to remain a problem for James himself.

One more quotation from the later preface should be added here, since it deals with what was to be a problem for James from the start, and often a source of criticism of his work:

Where, for the complete expression of one's subject, does a particular relation stop—giving way to some other not concerned in that expression? Really, universally, relations stop nowhere, the exquisite problem of the artist is eternally but to draw, by a geometry of his own, the circle within which they shall happily *appear* to do so. He is in the perpetual predicament that the continuity of things is the whole matter, for him, of comedy and tragedy; that this continuity is ever, but the space of an instant or an inch, broken, and that, to do anything at all, he has at once intensely to consult and intensely to ignore it.

It was this awareness that gained James the reputation of offering inconclusive conclusions, open-ended and indeterminate terminations, and a sense that while certain incidents or relations achieve their natural end or foreclosure, life is meanwhile streaming on, generating ever-new complexities. In this he was avoiding the endings of the popular novel in which the author felt he had the right, or obligation, to tie up all the loose ends and offer a conclusion in which everything was neatly concluded. Here again we can see James rebelling against the well-made popular novel in which the conventions of the form effectively concealed or dismissed the actual complexities of life.

## VI

*The American* (1877) is in many ways one of James's simpler works, since it is based on an almost schematic opposition between the American innocent—Christopher Newman could hardly be more obviously named—and some genuinely evil Europeans, the Bellegardes, who ruthlessly plot to prevent him from marrying their daughter, Claire de Cintré. The story is a mixture of melodrama and romance, a combination James was certainly due to use quite often, but perhaps never so blatantly or obviously. However, Newman is not simply an innocent: "It was our friend's eye that chiefly told his story; an eye in which innocence and experience were singularly blended." If he is amusingly inaccessible to the artistic heritage of Europe, he still has his own kind of knowledge, confidence, and even nobility. He was not contented by what America had to offer—"I seemed to feel a new man inside my old skin, and I longed for a new world." Though, as one character says of him, "You are the great Western Barbarian, stepping forth in his innocence and might, gazing a while at this poor effete Old World, and then swooping down on it." "Swooping" is not exactly what he does, but he has come on a determined search for a perfect wife—"My wife must be a magnificent woman." But his attitude to Europe does reveal something of his tough commercial past. "The world, to his sense, was a great bazaar, where one might stroll about and purchase handsome things; but he was no more conscious, individually of social pressure than he admitted the existence of such a thing as an obligatory purchase." But when he enters the home of the Bellegardes, "he had an unusual, unexpected sense of having wandered into a strange corner of the world. . . . For a moment he felt as if he had plunged into some medium as deep as the ocean, and as if he must exert himself to keep from sinking." And Madame de Cintré poses a special problem for him. "Newman wondered where, in so exquisite a compound, nature and art showed their dividing line. Where did the special intention separate from the habit of good manners? Where did urbanity end and sincerity begin?" The marquis is distinctly a more antipathetic figure—"a man of forms and phrases and postures; a man full of impertinences and treacheries."

What annoys the Bellegardes about Newman is that he has no sense of social hierarchy: "his sense of human equality was not an aggressive taste or an aesthetic theory, but something as natural and organic as a physical appetite which had never been put on a scanty allowance and consequently was innocent of ungraceful eagerness. His tranquil unsuspectingness of the relativity of his own place in the social scale was probably irritating to M. de Bellegarde. . . ." When, later, Newman enters the room of Madame de Cintré, who has been more than half won over to him, "he felt, as soon as he entered the room, that he was in the presence of something evil." She has in fact succumbed to the ruthless pressure and authority of her parents and agreed to renounce Newman. The Bellegardes cannot accept a "commercial person." Newman feels "sick, and suddenly helpless . . . to lose her by the interference and the dictation of others, by a impudent old woman and a pretentious fop stepping in with their 'authority'! It was too preposterous, it was too pitiful." But the power of the house is too strong for Madame de Cintré and she cannot break away: she has accepted the idea of becoming a nun (always a kind of living death in James). "The idea struck Newman as too dark and horrible for belief, and made him feel as he would have done if she had told him that she was going to mutilate her beautiful face, or drink some potion that would make her mad."

A kind of nausea sets in—"What a horrible rubbish heap of iniquity to tumble in!" Soon after, and here the plot becomes somewhat Gothic, Valentin de Bellegarde puts him in possession of an old secret which would effectively discredit, if not socially destroy, the Bellegardes. Newman is given a letter that incriminates the Bellegardes in murder. At first determined to have his revenge, Newman finally decides to let the whole matter go. The pages of the novel, in which James describes him coming to his decision, are curiously moving and quite transcend the Gothic mode. After going to look at the convent/prison of the Carmelites, in which Madame de Cintré is immured, he turns away, sad but relieved: "He turned away with a heavy heart, but with a heart lighter than the one he had brought. Everything was over, and he at last could rest." "Newman's last thought was that of course he would let the Bellegardes go. If he had spoken it aloud he would have said that he didn't want to hurt them. He was ashamed of having wanted to hurt them. They had hurt him, but such things were really not his game." He burns the damning letter, and his friend Mrs. Tristram comments with reference to the Bellegardes: "Their confidence, after counsel taken of each other, was not in their innocence, nor in their talent for bluffing things off; it was in your remarkable good nature! You see they were right."

The antiromantic conclusion of this novel disappointed many readers, including Howells himself. It seemed to violate the premises on which the narrative was set up, though we can see now that it was part of James's "realism" not to capitulate to the expected norms of the genre. In his later preface he offered a formulation that would fit many of his subsequent works: "Great and gilded the whole trap set, in fine, for his wary freshness and into which it would blunder upon its fate." As he confesses, the book is consummately "romantic," but without the conventional romantic resolutions. "Here then, at any rate, is the romantic *tout craché*— the fine flower of Newman's experience blooming in a medium 'cut off' and shut up to itself." In fact it was in this preface that James made a very important distinction which is relevant for all his work and worth quoting in full.

The real represents to my perception the things we cannot possibly *not* know, sooner or later, in one way or another; it being but one of the accidents of our hampered state, and one of the incidents of their quantity and number, that particular instances have not yet come our way. The romantic stands, on the other hand, for the things that, with all the facilities in the world, all the wealth and all the courage and all the wit and all the adventure, we never *can* directly know; the things that can reach us only through the beautiful circuit and subterfuge of our thought and desire.

And he goes on,

The only *general* attribute of projected romance that I can see, the only one that fits all its cases, is the fact of the kind of experience with which it deals—experience liberated, so to speak; experience disengaged, disembroiled, disencumbered, exempt from the conditions that we usually know to attach to it and, if we wish so to put the matter, draw upon it, and operating in a medium which relieves it, in a particular interest, of the inconvenience of a *related*, a measurable state, a state subject to all our vulgar communities. . . . The balloon of experience is in fact of course tied to the earth, and under that necessity we swing, thanks to a rope of remarkable length, in the more or less commodious car of the imagination; but it is by the rope we know where we are, and from the moment the cable is cut we are at large and unrelated: we only swing from the globe—though remaining as exhilarated, naturally, as we like, especially when all goes well. The art of the romancer is for the fun of it, insidiously to cut the cable, to cut it without our detecting him. What I have recognised then in *The American*, much to my surprise and after long years, is that the experience here represented is the disconnected and uncontrolled experience—uncontrolled by our general sense of "the way things happen"—which romance more or less successfully palms off on us.

As to what extent James's novels move toward pure romance as he describes it (cutting the cable "for the fun of it") that is something we have to decide individually: but we can readily see that much of his work operates from a tension between the "real," as here described, and the "romantic"; between the "earth" of unavoidably knowable reality and the "balloon" of romance, and "disconnected and uncontrolled experience." Perhaps no other writer derived so much, and so subtly, from operating between the earth of reality and the balloon of romance.

## VII

After the comparative disappointment of *The American*, James promised the *Atlantic* a novel that would better please its readers. This novel was *The Europeans* (1878) which varied James's basic narrative situation of bringing an American to Europe by bringing foreign characters to America. It concluded with no less than three happy marriages, though even then it failed to please his fellow countrymen, who found it weak or false in its local realism, while William James found it "insignificant." Yet it is without doubt a minor masterpiece in its own way, and deserves considered attention. We might say that in *The Europeans* there is a crucial question of "dress," which involved the problem of how the individual is to bear himself or herself in society. Writing of the National Portrait Gallery in 1897, James drew an interesting moral from the splendid pictures of the Tudor and Stuart groups: "This moral, startling perhaps in its levity, is simply the glory of costume, the gospel of clothes. From the ages of costume to the ages of none the drop is more than pitiful, and distinction is shattered by the fall. If you are to be represented, if you are to be perpetuated, in short, it is nothing that you be great or good—it is everything that you be dressed." This problematical relationship between aesthetic values and ethical values is close to the heart of James's work. For the notion of costume brings into question the status of all cultivated appearances. Is it immoral to devote energy to the adornment of surfaces? Is whatever is contrived to that extent also false? In a letter to William Dean Howells in 1877 James outlined the idea for the novel.

> I shall probably develop an idea that I have, about a genial, charming youth of a Bohemian father, who comes back from foreign parts into the midst of a mouldering and ascetic old Puritan family of his kindred . . . and by his gaiety and sweet

audacity smooths over their rugosities, heals their dyspepsia and dissipates their troubles. . . . It would be meant, roughly speaking, as the picture of the conversion of a dusty dreary domestic circle to epicureanism.

So much, "roughly speaking," is in the book, though the conversion is by no means complete. James had already explored the bewilderments and difficulties of the American trying to make his or her way through European territories saturated with culture and tradition, and he clearly found it comparably stimulating to imagine the progress of two quintessential Europeans through the comparatively blank spaces of America of the 1840s, and to depict not only their own intermittent bafflement and uncertainty, but also their impact on local Puritanism. It is worth noting that the main European of the book, Eugenia (well born), is not mentioned in James's outline. Without her, the ensuing confrontation of Puritan and European may well have been a little obvious. In adding her, James added immeasurably to the novel's depth and complexity; it now becomes a searching engagement of different values—values of costume and conduct—as well as a provocative encounter between different visions of life—life seen as discipline or opportunity.

From the start, the Europeans are connected with art and artifice. In the opening scene the rather obviously named Felix Young is drawing one of those effortless sketches that testify to his ability to extract pictorial values from the New World simply by accepting it with an uncritical serenity. Eugenia, characteristically restless because of a personal energy that as yet cannot find any expressive form, is looking in the mirror, checking her dress and the set of her hair. Through the window the visible landscape is unmitigatedly grim. It is in this bleak negative landscape that she is to try to find a place, a home. Perhaps the main question of the book is, can that colorless styleless landscape find room for her? She is from the beginning depicted as the careful mistress of her own person. She has many dresses and earrings which she wears "in alternation," and she is referred to as dark, foreign, exotic, with an Oriental aspect. She has, too, many names—Eugenia, Camilla, Dolores, the Baroness Münster, wife, through morganatic marriage, to the Prince of Silberstadt-Schreckstein. Her German name contains both wealth and fear. She is not simple, and her many names indicate a many-sidedness which raises suspicions among the Puritans who prefer character to be reduced to one clear facet and tonality. (On the other hand, the name of Felix Young is perhaps suspiciously too simple—is he *really* just the happy youth he always seems to be?) These two, Felix and Eugenia, are almost generic foreigners, now homeless and seeking to find a life and make their fortunes in the capaciousness of the New World. If this makes them seem like adventurers (as it does to most critics), it should also be noted how much they can contribute in the way of culture, costume, brilliant conversation, and an unfailing wit which testifies to an exhilarating play of mind. In addition, if Felix has a sort of genius for gaiety, Eugenia has a fine instinct for ceremony, often showing how an awkward unarranged event can be transformed into a graceful and civilized occasion. It is Eugenia, this veritable distillation of Europe, who comes to the home of her distant American relations and asks to be accommodated. "I should like to stay here. . . . Pray take me in." In the end they do not let her stay, and this is perhaps the book's most serious aspect, more serious than the fact that Felix does marry Gertrude and takes her away from the Puritan citadel of the Wentworths.

The virtues of the Wentworths are sufficiently intimated by their dwelling. White, still, clean, "lighter inside than it is out"—such is the house that Felix subsequently describes to Eugenia. She is, characteristically, keen to hear about the "accessories" and the "*mise en scène*," and he explains that the interior has "nothing for show, and very little . . . for the senses; but a great *aisance*, and a lot of money, out of sight." It is to this world without shades, colors, or concealments—except for money—that Eugenia presents herself. This overlit, underfurnished house is the very image of that pale, blank New England of the 1840s that James elsewhere describes as being composed of "high vertical moral light, the brightness of a society at once very simple and very responsible." The house is also, as so often in James, indicative of the mind inhabiting it. When Eugenia asks to be admitted to Mr. Wentworth's house, she is also asking to be admitted into the American consciousness of the time. But her advent is felt as a threat. "The sudden irruption into the well-ordered consciousness of the Wentworths of an element not allowed for in its scheme of usual obligations required a readjustment of that sense of responsibility which constituted its principal furniture." Mr. Wentworth cannot quite see Eugenia as part of his house; nor, indeed, can Eugenia herself. The decision to lodge her in a separate house "over the way" represents a compromise—hospitality without assimilation. It also keeps the threat of foreignness somewhat at bay. The young daughter, Gertrude, welcomes the idea: "It will be a foreign house." To which Mr. Wentworth replies: "Are we very sure that we need a foreign house?" Inevitably to him, as to others, Eugenia and Felix seem like a species of actors, mountebanks, who derive an immoderate pleasure from indulging in an irresponsible free play of the self made possible through words—and clothes, costumes, gestures. "I shall keep them in the other house," resolves Mr. Wentworth firmly. This, in effect, is the Puritan rejection of the expressive delights of style in favor of a few rigidly simple concepts of obligation and responsibility. When Felix asks Mr. Wentworth for the hand of Gertrude, he says that she needs a place in the world "that would bring her out." "A place to do her duty" counters Mr. Wentworth, thus implicitly revealing the opposition between self-exfoliation and self-contraction that lies at the heart of the book.

But America in this book is not simply the house of innocent dutiful purity, any more than Eugenia—for all her confessed "fibs," schemes, and simulations—is an incarnation of Old World duplicity and immorality. Mr. Wentworth's daughter Gertrude is as restless as Eugenia, and she too bridles at the church spires which menacingly confront her. Like Eugenia, she has an instinct for colorful clothes, and for the more exotic, Oriental side of life (she takes down the *Arabian Nights* while the others attend church). And it is Gertrude who brings out into the open one of the book's crucial issues when she cries out to the importunate clergyman Mr. Brand, concerning her relationship with Felix: "I am trying for once to be natural! . . . I have been pretending, all my life; I have been dishonest, it is you that have made me so!" The Puritans' self-conceit was that their way of life represented something nakedly simple and natural, whereas the amoral Europeans were given over to concealment and pretense. But here is a spirited child revealing that it is those honest, simple Puritans who have imposed a life of concealment and pretense on her, while it is with the adorned and eloquent Europeans that she feels most "natural." The paradox is a deep one: perhaps it is precisely with the aid of art that we may most readily discover, and be, our natural selves; while the attempt to deny and expunge art in the interests of purity and radical integrity may involve a falsification of the self far more destructive than the artifice in the flexible performance of the baroness, for instance. She is indeed effectively expelled, while the book dissolves in marriages; but this rejection reflects more damagingly on the limitations of the American consciousness that refuses to assimilate her and the civilizing influence she incorporates.

This limitation emerges most subtly in the figure of Robert Acton. He appears to have transcended the circumscriptions and suspicions of the Puritan mind: he has been a trader in the Orient and his house is full of good furniture and fine art. He seems relaxed, tolerant, and, above all, the only American in the book capable of appreciating Eugenia. But whereas Gertrude seeks true emancipation, Acton in his languorous worldliness is the reverse of emancipated. He is, for one thing, tied to his mother—a pale, ailing devotee of Emerson—as the last sentence of the book very prettily indicates. More palpably, there is a vitiating inertia about him: he is always seen lolling around with his hands in his pockets, leaning against things, as often as not lying down. This tendency to the supine state clearly indicates some more serious dearth of emotional energy. He is the worst kind of voyeur—curious, passionless. And Acton's attitude to Eugenia extends the paradox mentioned earlier in connection with Gertrude. Eugenia says she has come to America to enter into "natural relations," which she believes can flourish in America. In Europe, she confesses, there were only "artificial relations." Acton offers Eugenia the crude natural relation of becoming lovers, but as Eugenia says "that may be natural or not." Acton's typically Puritan notion of a brief and furtive indulgence in sex as constituting passion is not truly natural. In the end it is Acton who is really conventional and artificial in his conception of a relationship, and it is the supposedly artificial Eugenia who most understands what a truly natural relationship would be. Once again the American way is unexpectedly, and somewhat unpleasantly, the reverse of the natural way. Thus, early in his career James demonstrated his superior discernment by showing that the Puritan preoccupation with rigid rules of conduct may testify not to great passons manfully resisted, but simply to an absence of passion, and that "the great standard of morality" so often invoked may be only a rationalization for a great emotional anaesthesia.

In fact, Eugenia is almost too serious, too complex for the book. With her, as with none of the others, the possibilities of real suffering are envisaged. Eugenia begins to feel a "sense of the enlargement of opportunity" in the wild, American spaces; but then she learns that "the social soil on this big, vague continent was somehow not adapted for growing those plants she especially liked to inhale." Coming to America, like a wearied swimmer, she finds instead "a smooth, straight wall of rock." Certainly she has come to serve herself, perhaps save herself. But she does bring with her the seedlings of civilization to which the American soil proves innutritive; and the wall of rock which should have been a hospitable beach indicates as much a loss for America as it does a rebuff to Eugenia. Indeed, the implied comment on the Wentworths' America is curiously severe. Since Gertrude leaves in the name of naturalness and Eugenia is effectively excluded from it because of her arts, it becomes something of a problem to define exactly what does manage to flourish on that inhospitable soil. Certainly James seems here to suggest that art is indispensable for the liberation and expression of nature and, himself a supreme stylist, he can only deplore, in his humorous balanced way, the failure of this America gladly to accept and "take in" the natural stylishness of the Europeans. Finally, we should remember that Eugenia and Felix are themselves American in origin. They thus represent not some notional ideal European-ness, but rather versions of what Americans may become if they have been transplanted and "Europeanized." The novel therefore offers not a simple opposition of Americans versus Europeans, but instead a much subtler confrontation of two types of Americans: the sedentary, stay-at-homes and the culturally nomadic. Felix and Eugenia feel "a sacred satisfaction to have found a family" and as cousins, no matter how remote, they do literally belong to the American "family." They may seem morally more ambiguous than the Wentworths, but they are more complex and arguably richer civilized human beings. In refusing them (as Acton effectively "refuses" Eugenia) the American Americans may be seen as rejecting or disavowing some potentially enriching "relations."

Such a refusal of the chance to extend the American "family" to incorporate and appreciate its Europeanized relations (or its possible relationship to Europe) may fairly be seen as impoverishing.

## VIII

In the summer of 1878, while *The Europeans* was not amusing the readers of the *Atlantic, Daisy Miller* most distinctly was pleasing the readers of the English *Cornhill*. It came to be described as "an outrage on American girlhood" and enjoyed a success—or perhaps *succès de scandale*—which in retrospect seems somewhat disproportionate; but whatever else, it showed that James had hit upon a subject that fascinated his readers and that he would make his own—nothing less than "the American girl," endlessly simple, endlessly complex, who could say which? This is part of the charm, and enduring resonance, and the still-alive ambiguity of this deceptively simple tale. First of all, it is narrated by an American, who is rather stiff (he doesn't dance), rather too proper, too influenced by snobbish old ladies in his estimate of "the done thing," somewhat too effete in his rather shallow European veneer: he carries the appropriately chilly name of Winterbourne. When he meets Daisy, walking at large in their hotel in Vevey (Switzerland) he is immediately attracted, as, it seems, is she (we can never be sure with Daisy—we can only trust her, which Winterbourne ultimately, and perhaps fatally, fails to do). His descriptions of Daisy are a continuous oscillation, testifying to the fact that he cannot read this new kind of figure. (F. W. Dupee makes the important point that Daisy is not a product of Boston or of old New York, two different types of heroine who also play their part in James's work, but whose own kind of aristocratic breeding is more assured. Daisy is a daughter of the provincial plutocracy—Schenectady in the process of taking over New York—she is the American girl of the future.) Thus, at first, he has no doubts as he looks at her face: "this glance was perfectly direct and unshrinking. It was not, however, what would have been called an immodest glance, for the young girl's eyes were constantly moving," just as she is restless and likes a bit of a "fuss"— probably amounting to little more than a boat ride or a promenade with a suitable gentleman friend. But that constant facial movement puts her beyond any stable interpretation, and can worry Winterbourne as much as it can enchant him—more, perhaps. Winterbourne himself has become "dishabituated to the American tone"—another of those American expatriates who lose one set of cultural instincts without really gaining another. So he cannot work out whether Daisy is simply a pretty, social young woman: "or was she also a designing, an audacious, an unscrupulous young person? Winterbourne had lost his instinct in this matter. . . ." Indeed he has, and his direct appreciations start to turn into insidious suspicions. She is pronounced common by the self-appointed censors (Americans) of this provincial European society, but "it was a wonder to Winterbourne that, with her commonness, she had a singularly delicate grace." At times she seems to him "an extraordinary mixture of innocence and crudity." What she does reveal, in her own quiet way, and only when cornered, as it were, by overbearing negative advice, is a real spirit of independence: "I have never allowed a gentleman to dictate to me, or to interfere with anything I do."

This is the tone of the American woman of the future. Winterbourne, used to traditional "nice girls," finds her "an inscrutable combination of audacity and innocence." Winterbourne is not so inclined to damn her as the gossiping, cruel older Americans, who pride themselves on knowing what is delicate and indelicate, and try to hurt Daisy by cutting her in the crudest way. But when she is seen walking out alone with the gallant Italian Giovanelli, his faith in her begins to wane, though not without sympathy. "He was very sorry for her . . . because it was painful to hear so much that was pretty and undefended and natural assigned to a vulgar place among the categories of disorder." But she needs his faith more than pity. He continues to find her ambiguous: "He asked himself whether Daisy's defiance came from the consciousness of innocence, or from her being, essentially, a young person of the reckless class." The conclusion comes when Daisy insists on visiting the Colosseum by night, a place generally considered to be a miasmic spot where it was very easy to catch malaria (perhaps through some confusion with the miasma of history that had taken place there!). She is with Giovanelli, and Winterbourne, out walking, sees them together. From that point on he thinks "the riddle had become easy to read. She was a young lady whom a gentleman need no longer be at pains to respect." Effectively he drops her, and there is a hint that, in response, she simply abandons herself to the Roman fever which she subsequently contracts after her evening stroll through the polluted space of the old center of European civilization, and quickly dies. It is Giovanelli who speaks the most eloquent elegy—simple and doubt free. "She was the most beautiful young lady I ever saw, and the most amiable . . . and she was the most innocent." He has a trust and directness of insight that Winterbourne has lost. Daisy Miller, as a figure, has become part of the folklore of America, a figure, or a reference point, often cited in isolation from the fiction in which she figures. But we should note that the story is as much about Winterbourne and his indeterminate ambivalences as it is about her disturbingly attractive mixture of innocence, apparent recklessness, and innocent but strong spirit of independence.

Mention should be made here of Henry James's beloved young cousin Mary Temple who died while he was abroad in 1869–70. She was as brilliant, and changeable, and independent as Daisy Miller, and, in effect, James was to re-create her character in many figures in his fiction as the young American woman of the future. Many of his heroines, right up to Milly Theale (same initials) in *The Wings of the Dove*, may be related to his memories of the figure of Mary Temple, and many of his short stories—"An International Episode," "The Pension Beaurepas," "A Bundle of Letters," "The Patagonia," "The Last of the Valerii," "Madame de Mauves," "Four Meetings," for example—deal with international marriage, bright young American women discovering Europe, or American women whose free spirits bring them into some sort of trouble with the given social world, often represented by Europeans or Europeanized Americans, and in some ways these stories represent an interest in the American young woman that in part may be traced back to his devotion to Mary Temple. It has often been remarked that James seemed congenitally more sympathetic to the world and minds of women than of men, and despite his starting with Christopher Newman and Roderick Hudson, it remains true that he found more in the emerging female sensibility to engage his interest. In many ways, the world of men—particularly as equated with the world of business—was simply closed to him.

## IX

Published almost at the same time, *Washington Square* (1880) was a rather different kind of novel, with a very different kind of heroine. It is James's only novel named simply and directly after a place, and this gives us an opening clue. Catherine Sloper is the daughter of Dr. Sloper, and they reside in Washington Square: as the book develops the question is will she ever be able to escape Washington Square and all that it stands for in the way of coercive, restrictive paternal authority; and despite one joyless trip in Europe—mainly forced on her to teach her a lesson—the answer is that she does not. The story also revolves around money, and how it can pervert the possibilities of human relationships. Dr. Sloper thinks his daughter dull, plain, and stupid and, thus, at the mercy of any fortune hunter (she has a fortune from her mother and would inherit one from him). Thus, when the plausible, good-looking but essentially shallow and venal Morris Townsend enters her life, her father is quite determined to stop the match. If he is a clever, correct, and even just man, he is also a sadistic and ruthlessly cold one, bringing the abstract notions of geometry to bear on the delicacies and suffering of human feelings. He causes his daughter a great deal of pain—and he doesn't mind, as long as he keeps her from Morris Townsend. Meanwhile, Catherine's life is not being made any easier by the foolish meddlings of Dr. Sloper's sister, Mrs. Penniman, whose mind is soaked in romantic stereotypes and who attempts, as it were, to help the relationship of Catherine and Morris Townsend along the road of her fantasy: she had "a taste for light literature, and a certain foolish indirectness and obliquity of character. She was romantic; she was sentimental; she had a passion for little secrets and mysteries—a very innocent passion, for her secrets had hitherto been as unpractical as addled eggs." Catherine can see through her, and Morris finds her a bore when he discovers she cannot really help him in his plan, but her slightly wild romantic fantasying is to be put along with, or opposite to, her brother's cold calculating practicality if we are to comprehend the kind of "frame" within which Catherine has to operate.

Catherine, for all her apparent dullness, plainness, and shrinking modesty and fear of her father, is the most interesting and—

and it is part of James's genius that he can make us feel it—the most human and moving figure in the book. In her quiet way, she does indeed fall in love with Morris, who in his predictable way—the doctor is always right—takes himself off when he learns that the doctor will not leave Catherine his fortune if she marries him. She alone is the true lover who gives up everything for Morris and is willing to defy her father on his behalf. When they return from Europe—part of the father's plan to induce forgetfulness and fear through separation and solitude—we read "Catherine has brought home a present to every one—to every one save Morris, to whom she had brought simply her undiverted heart." That is arguably the greatest gift that one human being can give to another, but no one, and certainly not Morris, can appreciate its worth in the perverted money values and authority/fantasy patterns that dominate the world of Washington Square. Catherine abandons the idea of marriage, refuses Morris when he returns some years later—willing to settle for less. She takes her refuge in silence and stoical self-retraction: "It was almost the last outbreak of passion of her life; at least, she never indulged in another that the world knew anything about." Her father continues suspicious to the end, but Catherine has, in her own way, moved beyond his reach: "Catherine, however, became an admirable old maid. She formed habits, regulated her days upon a system of her own, interested herself in charitable institutions, hospitals, and aid societies; and went, generally, with an even and noiseless step, about the rigid business of her life. This life had, however, a secret history as well as a public one. . . . From her own point of view the great facts of her career were that Morris Townsend had trifled with her affection, and that her father had broken its spring. . . . There was something dead in her life, and her duty was to try to fill the void." But though she becomes somewhat old-fashioned, she is firm (she has her own kind of "unaggressive obstinacy"), and when Morris comes back she is not so easily to be picked up for her residual financial value: he is calmly and quietly, but quite definitively, sent packing. And the book ends with one of James's most perfectly modulated ironies: "Catherine, meanwhile, in the parlor, picking up her morsel of fancy-work, had seated herself with it again—for life, as it were." Just so; we have seen how this apparently unattractive, yet curiously moving girl, has been sentenced to Washington Square—for life, as it were.

## X

*Confidence* (also published in 1880) is a slighter work, though it perhaps doesn't deserve to have been dropped from the James canon in the way that it has. There are four main characters: the two men and the two young women representing very opposite types, though the story is not quite as symmetrical as this line-up of characters might suggest. Bernard Longueville is a rather feckless dandy who enjoys his own wit, who is "restless and professionless" and can go where he likes and say what occurs to him. He has no career, he simply enjoys himself. He "had the gift of sympathy—or at least was supposed to have it," but he is in fact basically a dilettante, self-amusing rover. His friend, Gordon Wright, apparently an honest upright man, has spent much time in German laboratories, but he lacks imagination, and when he thinks he is in love with Miss Vivian, he cannot trust his instincts but asks Bernard to come and "make a chemical analysis—a geometrical survey—of the lady of his love." She is a mysterious figure but he does not respond to this quality in her. "To be fascinated is to be mystified. Damn it, I like my liberty—I like my judgment." In a sense, neither man is fit to be in love—for Bernard it is just a game; for Gordon it is an experiment. Miss Vivian is enigmatic and mysterious—it is hard to sense what her feelings are. But when she realizes that Bernard has been asked by Gordon to come and experiment on her, while he (Gordon) goes away, she responds with a suitable inscrutability. She is not willing to be made the object of an experiment. The fourth figure is Miss Blanche Evers, who is taken by Bernard simply to be "the American pretty girl" with her endless slightly silly chatter about people, shops, and places. When Bernard has tested Miss Vivian—part of the experiment—and Gordon comes back, Bernard, for complex motives, returns a negative verdict, indicating that he does not think she is a suitable match for his friend.

This verdict may or may not be disinterested—Bernard seems to be falling in love with Miss Vivian. In any case, Miss Vivian refuses Gordon who immediately goes away. He then marries Blanche Evers who, despite her foolish chatter, obviously cares for him. Bernard gets engaged to Miss Vivian, seemingly having felt love for the first time. Then Gordon returns, feels he has been tricked by his friend, and asks Miss Vivian for another chance (i.e., he will get divorced if necessary). But Miss Vivian can see that he is, in fact, "intensely in love with his wife," and that his claim for another chance is quite pointless. In response to Bernard's questioning about her behavior she says: " 'You certainly made a study of me—and I was determined you should get your lesson wrong. I determined to embarrass, to mislead, to defeat you. Or rather, I didn't determine; I simply obeyed a natural impulse of self-defiance—the impulse to evade the fierce light of criticism. I wished to put you all in the wrong.' " This she effectively does. Gordon goes back to his wife with a new appreciation of her, and Bernard realizes what it really is to be in love—as he is with Miss Vivian. The quartet have matched up, though in rather odd ways, as no one is quite what he or she seems.

Here we should note the title—*Confidence*—for this poses the great problem of relationships. Early, Angela Vivian says: " 'There was never anything like mamma's confidence. I am very different; I have no confidence. And then I don't like being deposited, like a parcel, or being watched, like a curious animal. I am too fond of my liberty. . . . I have no confidence—none whatever, in anyone or anything.' " Here is the problem—if a woman is fond of her liberty and sees and feels men plotting and experimenting and observing all around her, how shall she come to feel any confidence in them? On the contrary, an intelligent suspicion would seem to be the appropriate vigilance, and that is what Miss Vivian exhibits for most of the book. She is not enigmatic, but simply on her guard among basically selfish people. As to Gordon's rushing off to test her, Bernard says this was "the last proof of his confidence," to which Angela replies, "It was not a proof of confidence. . . . It had nothing to do with me. It was as between himself and you; it was a proof of independence." And when she does accept the bantering, uncertain Bernard, she simply says—"I have confidence." The novel, then, does resolve itself in unexpected symmetries—but the key word is "confidence," for without that there can be no true relationships, only games, jokes, experiments, and selfish surveys of presumptive intent. Miss Vivian is quiet because she knows that the one necessary thing is confidence, and until she finds it and feels it she will only spoil the game, break the joke, and foul up the experiment. In this she is a crucial, if minor, Jamesian figure—she wants her liberty, and will only surrender it when she feels proper confidence in the intentions and feelings of another. That problem of liberty for one-self, and confidence in another, is to run all through James's work: confidence in the self can make for freedom; confidence in another is necessary for love and lasting relationships—can the two kinds of confidence be joined without sacrificing one to the other? Here is a typical Jamesian problem.

## XI

Also published at this time was James's most important work of literary criticism, his book on Hawthorne. One of his intentions in this work was to show off his own Englishness and "European-ness"—with comparisons to Balzac and Thackeray—by stressing and overstressing the provinciality of America and Hawthorne (and most other American writers mentioned in the book—Emer-son, Thoreau, Poe). In a famous review of the book, William Dean Howells made some fair objections in his usual temperate way: "If it is not provincial for an Englishman to be English, or a Frenchman French, then it is not for an American to be American; and if Hawthorne was 'exquisitely provincial,' one had better take one's chance of universality with him than with almost any Londoner or Parisian of the time." James had adopted an oppo-site point of view at the very outset of his book by affirming that "the moral is that the flower of art blooms only where the soil is deep, that it takes a great deal of history to produce a little litera-ture, that it needs a complex machinery to set a writer in motion." He did not believe that "human life" was some abstract essence that could be seen and grasped in separation from the diverse forms through and among which it manifested itself. And these forms were, simply, society. "We know a man imperfectly until we know his society," he said in a later essay on Emerson. The richer and denser the society, the greater the number of potential sources of knowledge. James's case against America was not based on any notion that it was somehow intellectually backward or morally inferior to Europe (rather the contrary indeed); it was instead that, as a novelist, he found it comparatively empty. In that same essay on Emerson (1887) James spoke of the curious fate of "the primitive New England character" and "its queer search for something to expend itself upon." If you consider that character and the thin society in which it had its being, James went on, you get "the impression of a conscience gasping in the void, panting for sensations, with something of the movement of a landed fish." Where America was a void, Europe was a plenitude, or, to follow his own imagery, it was an ocean in which the gasping American conscience could at least find an element to swim in. That a person, particularly an American, might well drown in those deep and dangerous waters was a part of James's sense of the complexity of the American fate. But as a novelist he clearly felt that there was more to be learned from a swimming fish than from a landed one.

To establish this image of a genius starved for adequate material to work on, James quotes passages in which Hawthorne depicts his plight in just this way. Thus: "no author, without a trial, can conceive of the difficulty of writing a romance about a country where there is no shadow, no antiquity, no mystery, no picturesque and gloomy wrong, nor anything but a commonplace prosperity, in broad and simple daylight, as is happily the case in my dear native land." And again: "I have another great difficulty in the lack of materials; for I have seen so little of the world that I have nothing but thin air to concoct my stories of. . . ." And having established the picture of a genius starved in America, James goes on to imply that when Hawthorne did get to Europe he was too old to take advantage of what it offered. Thus, commenting on Hawthorne's book on England (*Our Old Home*), James says: "It is the work of an outsider, of a stranger, of a man who remains to the end a mere spectator (something less even than an observer), and always lacks the initiation into the manners and nature of a people of whom it may be said, that to know them is to make discoveries."

The implication is clear: James himself had come to an early realization of the paucity of material in America and had removed himself to Europe at the right age to partake of what he later called "the banquet of initiation." In such ways do we see James quietly justifying and defining his own position while sympathetically outlining the difficulties Hawthorne faced as an artist in America. There are many contradictions in the book, as James oscillates between his desire to put a distance between himself and Hawthorne, and a realization that, as a writer, he was much closer to Hawthorne than he had allowed. For instance, on the one hand, James effectively deprecates Hawthorne's work by continually attaching to it such epithets as "charming," "exquisite," "soft," "simple," "pure," "natural," "spontaneous," "childlike," and so on—as though to emphasize that Hawthorne's work was as innocent and simple as the land it emerged from (the epithets seem very incongruous and inapposite to us now). On the other hand, many of his most brilliant comments reveal that he was far from unaware of the troubling depths in Hawthorne's work, as when he says of Hawthorne's imagination that it was "always engaged in a game of hide-and-seek in the region in which it seemed to him that the game could best be played—among the shadows and substructions, the dark based pillars and supports of our moral nature." He credits Hawthorne, rightly, with "a haunting care for moral problems" and sums up by saying, "Man's conscience was his theme." Such penetrating insights as these reveal that James was at least half aware of those elements that were carried over into his own work; for most of the above remarks (after the patronizing words about "soft" and "childlike") would perfectly fit James's own fiction. Similarly, he speaks disparagingly of Hawthorne's use of symbols and allegory, for this was the period when James was still trying to emulate the great European realists. Yet he allowed that Hawthorne's allegories offered "glimpses of a great field, of the whole deep mystery of man's soul and conscience. . . . The fine thing in Hawthorne is that he cared for the deeper psychology." Nothing about childlike spontaneity here—this is the great American writer whose symbolic and allegorical power, and care for "the deeper psychology," would increasingly reappear in the work of James. And sometimes, indeed, the deeply understanding sympathy reveals itself in memorable words, as when he compares Hawthorne to Emerson: "Emerson, as a sort of spiritual sun-worshipper, could have attached but a moderate value to Hawthorne's cat-like faculty of seeing in the dark." It was just such a faculty, rather than any British or European mastery of the concretions of society, that would make James what he was to become—an unmistakably great, and an unmistakably American, novelist—a novelist who, as this little book beautifully if unconsciously reveals, owed his greatest debt not to Balzac but to Nathaniel Hawthorne.

## XII

James could now finally set to work on *The Portrait of a Lady*, which was intended as a culmination of his work to date, and was meant also to establish him as a major writer who could avail himself of the strengths of both the European and American traditions of fiction, while developing the international theme, which he had effectively made his own. It had something of the success it deserved in both countries (serialized by *Macmillans* in London and the *Atlantic* in America), and we can see quite clearly now that it is one of James's most notable masterpieces and one of the really major works of the nineteenth century. The story in outline is familiar enough no doubt: once more James sends an innocent young American woman to Europe—the starting point, he says, was "the conception of a certain young woman affronting her destiny" (notice "affront" not "confront"—there is a certain haughty insolence in Isabel Archer as she *overconfidently*—we see how important the word is in James—takes on her destiny, with a fine disregard for the problematics of such an undertaking). Once in Europe she is variously proposed to, planned around, and plotted against: she is made rich by a bequest, and this simply adds to the dangerous illusion of a high-sailing freedom.

As it turns out, she makes a disastrous marriage to a perverted asthete, a Europeanized American named Osmond (the name has a dead skeletal ring—the bone/the world), acting in collaboration with his ex-lover, Madame Merle, another highly elegant, deeply treacherous Europeanized American (the dangers in this book, and the deepest immoralities, do not come from Europeans—James is far beyond the unsubtle polarity of American innocence ensnared by European immorality and guile: the perverted American is the real danger). Much of the book traces the slow process by which Isabel comes to realize how she has simply been used in a scheme by the two Americans, a realization that culminates in one of the great passages in James as she sits by the fire late into the night, going over what has happened to her, and just where she really is. As James says of the passage in his Preface to the novel: "she sits up, by her dying fire, far into the night, under the spell of recognitions on which she finds the last sharpness suddenly wait. It is a representation simply of her motionlessly *seeing*, and an attempt withal to make the mere still lucidity of her act as 'inter-

40

esting' as the surprise of a caravan or the identification of a pirate." As any reader will agree, it is much *more* interesting than any number of caravans and pirates and is one of the high points to which psychological fiction reached. Isabel finally makes an effective breach with her husband by going to see her dying cousin, Ralph, who has always loved her in his own disabled fraternal way. But, despite the urgings of her strong American suitor, Caspar Goodwood, at the end of the book she seems to be returning to her sterile marriage in Rome. The ambiguous ending has vexed some readers, but it is appropriate for the haughty woman who affronted her fate, and was herself affronted by it.

It is a magnificent book—James had never yet written so majestically or with so much easy confidence. Nor had he ever been so fully in control of his material. The novel defies summary, but certain points about its themes can be mentioned. From Isabel's point of view the book is about the dream of pure space, and the subsequent experience of contaminated limitations. She speaks the language of theoretical freedom, but experiences the actuality of malign intentions. She holds on to her idea of acting in pure freedom for as long as possible, a sort of deluded existentialist who believes in absolutely unconditioned free choice. But in fact she is constantly tampered with: Mrs. Touchett "brings her out," Ralph plans with his father to give her money as a sort of experiment to see what she will do, and, of course, Osmond and Madame Merle plot around her and use her. In answer to Ralph's comment on his mother—"She has adopted you"—she answers—"I'm not a candidate for adoption" and "I'm very fond of my liberty," like many American heroes from Huck Finn to Augie March. In an important scene in St. Paul's she says, "The world comes to strike one as rather small," and James adds, "This attitude was part of a system, a theory, that she had lately embraced." She seeks to live by her own systems and theories, not considering that other people may have their own. She insists on choice—"I wish to choose my fate"—whereas it will be mostly chosen for her by the disregarded (by Isabel) intentionality of other people. Her "love of liberty," says James, "was as yet almost exclusively theoretical"—she is not versed in the praxis of the world. Osmond deceives her by pretending to share her own attitude to her position, saying "you can do exactly what you choose; you can roam through space."

This is an abiding American dream; but all the time she is moving into a prison composed of other people's plots. Miltonic echoes are brought in: "The world lay before her—she could do whatever she chose." But she enters what the Countess Gemini calls "a steel trap" under the illusion that she is extending her freedom. She is of course *too* theoretic, and thus unprepared for the facticity of the world. She has her system: but everybody else has his or her own system, and wary as she is of getting involved in anybody else's system—an abiding American dread—she in fact involves herself in the most constricting, life-denying system of all. When Madame Merle criticizes her for not succeeding in the plan to marry Pansy (her daughter by Osmond—a secret not known to Isabel for some time) to Warburton, a wealthy English lord, Isabel reflects "that there was more intention in her past behaviour than she had allowed for at the time. Ah yes, there had been intention, there had been intention, Isabel said to herself; and she seemed to wake from a long pernicious dream . . . a strange truth was filtering into her soul." The movement of the book is thus from a theory of some kind of transcendent freedom in empty space to an experience of the world's crowdedness, and a confrontation of the fact that the encircling psyches of other people all have "intentions" (a key word in the book). Indeed, consciousness depends on "intentionality" (see the work of the phenomenologists), and intentions can lead to plots and the desire to use other people to amplify or realize a personal system or theory. Isabel falls victim to the theory of Osmond about the relation of art to life and as a consequence is nearly dehumanized—immersed in the unsuspected malign intentionality of a person in whom she has too much confidence (as, initially, she has in herself).

James is very clear about how he saw Isabel Archer, as we can see from his Introduction. "I had my vivid individual," he says, "vivid, so strangely, in spite of being still at large, not confined by conditions, not engaged in the tangle to which we look for much of the impress that constitutes an identity." Without that impress, from which Isabel feels so privilegedly free, there can be no identity; one of the things that Isabel acquires from her great mistake is indeed an identity. To provide that tangle, James said he found it came to "organising an ado about Isabel Archer." So around her "perfect isolation," and penetrating it, James duly establishes a highly complex ado of many variants. The uncommitted self has to commit itself in the interests of acquiring an identity. With notable exceptions, to remain in pure potential is to be nothing actual.

So Isabel has to choose. But why does she seem to make such a disastrously wrong choice? We may say that at first her preconceptions interfere with her perceptions. She says of her first impressions of England that it is like a novel, a pantomime, a picture made real. Fictional and aesthetic images come before, and often regulate, her reading of the real thing. We are told of her early education, reading German transcendental philosophy, which is perhaps not the best preparation for assessing and living in the imperfect actual world. She is also an "egoist"; she has theories about her own nature which she compares to a garden: she likes to wander around in her "remarkable soul" gathering roses. This suggests a dangerous, self-worshipping solipsism, so self-absorbed as to ignore the reciprocities of life. She has intimations that "there were other gardens in the world . . . a great many places that were not gardens at all—only dusky pestiferous tracts, planted thickly with ugliness and misery." And indeed, her rose-filled garden is surrendered to, and mastered by, the sterile waste-land of Osmond's inner life. She chooses his system of life, having rejected other, more humane ones. When Warburton pays attention to her "she felt that a territorial, a political, a social magnate had conceived the design of drawing her into the system in which he rather invidiously lived and moved." Her instinct is to resist, desist we might say, for she feels that "virtually she had a system and an orbit of her own." Caspar Goodwood has "no system at all" (the unsocialized American male, direct but crude). Isabel thinks she can move between no system and other peoples' systems. But this is an illusion. She lives by ideals and images, i.e., she measures life up to her ideal theory, rather than checking the theory against life. And life is usually found wanting. Notice that this can be an excuse for refusing life. When she feels Warburton is about to propose, she wishes "both to elude the intention and satisfy her curiosity," one of the most telling comments on her as a voyeur who wishes to avoid participation. As Ralph says to her "you want to see, but not to feel."

It may be that part of Osmond's secret attraction for Isabel (nobody else is remotely taken in by his posing) is that she senses that he promises a passionless life; that in his talk of "making life a work of art" she realizes that she can become part of his collection, a sort of escape from the mire and fury of human life by an act of self-reification. The lady would, as it were, rather be a portrait—and that is what she seems to become as she helps to keep up the masquerade of the "magnificent form"—as Osmond thinks of it—of their marriage. We should note that in the everyday world her most common emotion is fear. She is frightened of Caspar's sexual drive, or assertive virility; of Warburton's social system; she is frightened of her money; and she is frightened of herself. The money forces her into the world in which, as Mrs. Touchett says, she must "play the part" and "take care of [her] things"—i.e., she is now obliged to be aware of the obligations of performance and possession. And Isabel reacts by saying "I'm afraid" three times. By choosing Osmond, who *says* that his one vocation is "my wilful renunciation" (as we quickly realize he is in fact the most worldly of men), Isabel thinks she is opting for a life lived at the high level of the ideal. But from another point of view she is trying to escape from the world—the complexities of its systems, the pressures of its passions.

Madame Merle—the blackbird—is Osmond's partner in plotting, and she has acquired such an apparently civilized veneer that Isabel is still American enough to feel she is "not natural." Yet in many ways she wishes to emulate Madame Merle's total self-control and cool detachment (Madame Merle's most chilling remark is "I don't pretend to know what people are for. . . . I only know what I can do with them"). These two ladies have one exchange that is crucial to the book. It starts when Isabel says that she does not care what kind of house Caspar Goodwood has. Madame Merle's answer is central. " 'That's very crude of you. When you've lived as long as I have you'll see that every human being has his shell and that you must take the shell into account. By the shell I mean the whole envelope of circumstances. There's no such thing as an isolated man or woman; we're each of us made up of some cluster of appurtenances. What shall we call our 'self'? Where does it begin? Where does it end? It overflows into everything that belongs to us—and then it flows back again. I know a large part of myself is the clothes I choose to wear. I've a great respect for *things*! One's self—for other people—is one's expression of one's self; and one's house, one's furniture, one's garments, the books one reads, the company one keeps—these things are all expressive.' " Now, there is a great deal in this that is true, but Isabel immediately disagrees. " 'I don't agree with you. I think just the other way. I don't know whether I succeed in expressing myself, but I know that nothing can express me; everything's on the contrary a limit, a barrier, and a perfectly arbitrary one. Certainly the clothes which, as you say, I choose to wear, don't express me; and heaven forbid they should. . . . My clothes may express the dressmaker, but they don't express me. To begin with it's not my own choice that I wear them; they're imposed upon me by society.'

'Should you prefer to go without them?' Madame Merle enquired in a tone which virtually terminated the discussion."

Isabel is very American in her suspicion of "things" as "limits" and her idea of a pure self existing apart from all materiality. But without limits you cannot have identity. And while the self is not *identical* with things, Madame Merle is right to the extent that the self must enter into commerce with things (houses, clothes, other people, etc.) to establish itself as a self and experience itself as a self. There is no self in a void. The danger, of course, is when things absorb the self, and the self abandons itself to thinghood. Isabel is dangerously one-sided—and vulnerable—in what she thinks of as her contempt for the encircling things that make up her world as much as they do anybody else's.

It is partly this error that brings her into Osmond's "prison" while she thought she had been discovering her liberty. As she says to herself in the great night meditation: "she had taken the first steps in the purest confidence, and then she had suddenly found the infinite vista of a multiplied life to be a dark, narrow alley with a dead wall at the end . . . he had led her into the mansion of his own habitation, then, *then* she had seen where she really was. . . . Between those four walls she had lived ever since; they were to surround her for the rest of her life. It was the house of darkness, the house of dumbness, the house of suffocation. . . . When she saw this rigid system close about her, draped though it was in pictured tapestries, that sense of darkness and suffocation of which I have spoken took possession of her; she seemed shut up with an odour of mould and decay." Isabel—with her own system, her theory of freedom, has been engorged and trapped by Osmond's more rigid system which seeks to make over other people for his own use, transforming them into things for his manipulation (as he does with his daughter Pansy). Isabel's crime is "having a mind of her own." He cannot tolerate the otherness of free-standing people.

It is part of the characteristic atmosphere of the book that, while Isabel develops in her own way and sight deepens into insight, there is a growing feeling of free spontaneous life giving way, or turning into, mechanistic automata, art objects, instruments, masks, theatrical performances, shells containing no life. People become dry and empty, touched or blighted with that desiccation that for Shakespeare was a mark of evil or dead life— as when Madame Merle complains to Osmond, "you've dried up my soul." Even Isabel, near the end, goes into something like a catatonic state, devoid of "purpose [and] intention," envying statues and objects their insentient immobility, longing, even, for death. In particular, this mood afflicts her as she is on her way to see Ralph who is dying—she has gone against Osmond's express desire that she shouldn't, but to her he scarcely exists as a human being any more. And to Ralph, arguably the one true lover in the book, she finally comes, and a moving deathbed scene ensues. "She had lost all her shame, all wish to hide things. Now he must know; she wished him to know, for it brought them supremely together." When she says she would die not to lose him he answers: "You won't lose me—you'll keep me. Keep me in your heart. I shall be nearer to you than I've ever been. Dear Isabel, life is better; for in life there's love. Death is good—but there's no love." And he ends by assuring her "if you've been hated you've also been loved. Ah but, Isabel—*adored!*" And in a moment of recognition of her truest allegiance she answers, "Oh my brother!"

The final exchange is with Caspar. She is sitting on an old bench in the garden, which will become the bench of meditation and the bench of desolation in James's later work. She feels "a singular absence of purpose. . . . There was nothing to recall her to the house." By this time the garden/house contrast has taken on many ambiguous connotations: among other things, the garden is the garden of interiority, the withdrawn consciousness, while the house is, in its various forms, the house of life, and active participation in the social game. Caspar speaks to Isabel in a language she would once have agreed with. "It's too late to play a part;

didn't you leave all that behind you in Rome? . . . Why should you go back?—why should you go through that ghastly form. . . . We can do absolutely as we please; to whom under the sun do we owe anything? . . . The world's all before us—and the world's very big." Almost all these ideas and propositions she has voiced in the past. Now he is the spokesman of new beginnings, of the world as possibility, of the casting off of dead forms (he sees that what Osmond insists is a "magnificent form" is, in fact, a "ghastly form"). The appeal is very strong and, for once, the virginal Isabel Archer succumbs to a kiss—the only one, at least, that we are told of. And at this moment the world around her seems "to take the form of a mighty sea, where she floated in fathomless waters." She feels herself drawn to the idea of sinking in his arms, in pure passion: but she also feels herself threatened by this liquidity. It is not the way for her, and the kiss seems to "free her from this pull." "She never looked about her; she only darted from the spot. There were lights in the windows of the house; they shone far across the lawn. In an extraordinarily short time . . . she had moved through the darkness (for she saw nothing) and reached the door. Here only she paused. She looked all about her. She had not known where to turn; but she knew now. There was a very straight path."

This has been taken as a form of spiritual suicide, of perverse and masochistic renunciation of a genuine chance for a new start—for, where does that "very straight path" lead to? James, teasingly—maddeningly to some—does not say. But there is a realism in this last gesture of that strange and fearful woman, Isabel Archer. She has no belief in a recoverable freedom, a freedom that was initially purely theoretic. We are what we have done, and what has been done to us. Isabel, who has always been frightened of passion and the oceanic tug of released feelings, returns to the form, the play. For another character, that doorway might lead to adultery, or it might lead to a life of the artist—as James's door had led him to. And both topics occur quite frequently in his later work. Here, however, Isabel goes back, so we feel, to Rome and the ruins of her life (and perhaps to save Pansy from Osmond's malignity—which she alone can do), but she has acquired a new consciousness of the whole situation, a new awareness of the world. She has had to face the fact that she has been used as a thing—"a woman who has been made use of"—and finally see "the dry staring fact that she had been an applied handled hung-up tool, as senseless and convenient as mere shaped wood and iron." And she must live with that knowledge—though such knowledge brings with it a larger knowledge of life itself. She will no longer be a victim of Osmond's rigid system, nor indeed of anyone else's. At last, we feel, she will be her own woman, appreciating the part and place she must take in the world.

At this moment of triumph James is thirty-eight, with thirty-five more years of writing ahead of him, during which time he will make many more experiments and innovations in "the art of fiction." Since these are for James "the middle years," we may conclude this section with a quotation from the story of that title (though it was not written until 1893). There the dying Dencombe announces with almost his last words: "A second chance—*that's* the delusion. There never was to be but one. We work in the dark—we do what we can—we give what we have. Our doubt is our passion and our passion is our task. The rest is the madness of art." James did, however, have endless chances— he made them for himself by his uncompromising devotion to his craft. What that dedication to "the madness of art" was to produce in later years will be considered in subsequent chapters.

# II

## London, 1882–1898:

## "The Compendium of the World"

N NOVEMBER 1881, Henry James was sitting in a Boston hotel. He had returned to America, while *The Portrait of a Lady* was nearing its conclusion in the magazines, out of a sudden desire to renew direct contact with his family. "I needed to see again *les miens*, to revive my relations with them, and my sense of the consequences that these relations entail." As it turned out he had returned only to see them die, and America itself seemed barren, alien, and innutrient. While he was sitting in that Boston hotel—it was still prior to the deaths of his parents—he embarked on an extraordinary summing up of his life so far, which he committed to his notebook. It is a mixture of retrospective definition and prospective intention and flows on for pages as Henry James not only takes stock of his position but also clarifies to himself what it was to be Henry James at that moment. There is space only for some select extracts. (Incidentally, and perhaps oddly, he got his own age wrong —he was thirty-eight.)

> I am 37 years old, I have made my choice, and God knows that I have now no time to waste. My choice is the old world—my choice, my need, my life. My work lies there—and with this vast new world, *je n'ai que faire*. One can't do both—one must choose. No European writer is called upon to assume that ter-

49

rible burden. The burden is necessarily greater for an American—for he *must* deal, more or less, even if only by implication, with Europe; whereas no European is obliged to deal in the least with America. . . . The painter of manners who neglects America is not thereby incomplete as yet; but a hundred years hence—fifty years hence perhaps—he will doubtless be accounted so.

James goes on to recall his many European experiences and then comes to the moment he decided to move to London. Since it was in many ways the most important decision of his life, I will quote again from the notebook.

I don't remember what suddenly brought me to the point of saying—"Go to; I will try London." I think a letter from William had a good deal to do with it, in which he said, "Why don't you?—That must be the place." . . . I *did* try it, and it has succeeded beyond my most ardent hopes. I came to London as a complete stranger, and today I know much too many people. *J'y suis absolument comme chez moi.* Such an experience is an education—it fortifies the character and embellishes the mind. It is difficult to speak adequately or justly of London. It is not a pleasant place; it is not agreeable, or cheerful, or easy, or exempt from reproach. It is only magnificent. . . . You may call it dreary, heavy, stupid, dull, inhuman, vulgar at heart and tiresome in form. I have felt these things at times so strongly that I have said—"Ah London, you too then are impossible?" But these are occasional moods; and for one who takes it as I take it, London is on the whole the most possible form of life. I take it as an artist and a bachelor; as one who has the passion of observation and whose business is the study of human life. It is the biggest aggregation of human life—the most complete compendium of the world. The human race is better represented there than anywhere else, and if you learn to know your London you learn a great many things.

So London it was to be—for the next sixteen years, with few interruptions (a visit to Paris in 1884 where he again met and talked to Zola, Daudet, Edmond de Goncourt; a long stay in Italy in 1886–87 which generated a number of his greatest stories, including "The Aspern Papers"). He was to meet most of the well-known writers of the time—Tennyson, Browning, George Eliot—and many social celebrities, including Gladstone. Indeed in one winter he dined out 107 times. He was certainly getting to know his compendium! In the end he was to withdraw—retreat, perhaps—from it, exhausted and disappointed. But that is a later story. In 1882 James's visit to America was darkened by the death of his mother in January of that year. He returned to London, but was almost immediately recalled by the news that his father was dying.

After the loss of his parents—*les miens* were no more—Henry James settled in London (first near Piccadilly, then to Kensington) and, immensely productive, entered into a new phase of his writing career. Indeed, James's sojourn in London was to take him through three distinct phases. Having, as he thought, somewhat exhausted the "international theme," he turned away from his Daisy Millers and Isabel Archers and embarked on what were intended to be serious social novels in what was then thought of as the naturalist mode. The three major ones were *The Bostonians, The Princess Casamassima* (both published in 1886), and *The Tragic Muse* (1890). They were all pretty much failures with the public and James felt he had to try something else. He turned to writing drama for some five years (1890–95). Here he failed even more seriously. A dramatization of *The American* had a little success, but on the first night of *Guy Domville* Henry James came out to take a bow after the play was over, only to be booed and jeered by an angry audience.

Much has been made of this incident, and given James's sensibility there is no doubt that it was in certain ways traumatic. After this disaster he returned to fiction, but the fiction takes a new turn. It is constantly experimental, not only drawing on what he had learned from writing for the theater, but also exploiting in new ways such strange genres as the ghost story ("The Turn of the Screw" is perhaps the most famous). He also wrote a number of tales about unsuccessful writers and artists, and stories of spoilt childhoods, contaminated innocence, blighted adolescence. He was undoubtedly going through some sort of crisis in his career, and it reflects itself in a number of strange, devious works, full of moral dubieties and unusual, even perverse, psychological processes and behaviors taking place in a social atmosphere that is darkening, at times toxic, mephitic. James's attitude to London had grown more sombre—by which I am also saying that his attitude to life had as well, since what, for James, was life, if it was not London? Feeling estranged from his adopted city and unappreciated and unwanted by his audience, James left London and finally purchased an old house with a walled garden in Rye, Sussex. This was Lamb House where he went in 1898, and where he was to write his final masterpieces. But that is another story, and we must turn now to James's writings during his London years.

## II

"I wished to write a very *American* tale, a tale very characteristic of our social conditions, and I asked myself what was the most salient and peculiar point in our social life. The answer was: the situation of women, the decline of the sentiment of sex, the agitation on their behalf." Thus James formulates to himself the generative idea of his novel *The Bostonians*. He set about depicting a group of Bostonian women concerned, in different ways and to different degrees, with the cause of feminism—or redressing the wrongs done to women by men over the centuries. The central member of this group is Olive Chancellor, who is hysterically bigoted in her commitment to "the cause" and obsessively, pathologically unremitting in her total aggression toward men. She takes up a young girl, adopting her—indeed effectively "buying" her from her venal, fraudulent parents (the father a charlatan faith healer, the mother a vapid foolish would-be social climber). The girl, Verena Tarrant, is another of those slightly magical innocent young women who appear through James's fiction—vulnerable and yet firm; malleable and yet essentially themselves; timid and yet daring; at times loving and yet somehow unreachable; capable of deep silences and long looks and unexpected declarations; innocent and yet with some nameless knowledge all their own. Sometimes almost a blank, such figures are nevertheless often the magnetic center of the works in which they appear. And so it is with Verena Tarrant. She has some sort of gift for apparently impromptu "inspired" public utterance—long persuasive speeches about the sufferings and rights of women. And yet the words do not seem to come from her—she is a passive vehicle for a discourse not her own. As we say now, she does not really speak on such occasions—she is spoken.

Olive Chancellor appropriates Verena Tarrant, partly to de-

velop her gift to further the feminist cause, and partly because—
although she hardly recognizes it—she is intensely, deviantly, and
perversely in love with her. James noted that his book "should be
a study of one of those friendships between women which are so
common in New England." It is irrelevant and limiting to consider it as a study of lesbianism. James is considering a much
larger matter—the perversion (it is a common word in the book)
of sexuality and emotionality, the confusion and debasement of
relationships, the aberrant and extreme ideologists of "the masculine" and "the feminine," "the decline of the sentiment of sex"
as James ambiguously puts it—which all pervade the book and
which are signs, simply, of a society gone wrong. The drama of the
book is precipitated by the arrival in Boston of a distant cousin of
Olive Chancellor's—a man named Basil Ransom who is something of a refugee from the ravaged post–Civil War South. He is
almost as extreme in his ideas about the respective roles and
places of men and women as Olive is in her hysterical denuncia-
tions of his sex. He falls in love with Verena and from then on it is
war, almost to the death, between him and Olive as to which of
them should possess her. In giving up, temporarily, the international theme, James had not given up the organization of his work
around complex oppositions. Instead of America and Europe, we
now have the differences between the North and the South in
America, and even more important, an exploration of the most
crucial and ambiguous (not to say controversial) difference of
them all—between male and female.

The note of deviancy and perversion is pervasive and touches
nearly all the characters in different ways: it is as though no one is
sure what constitutes his or her identity, what his or her place is in
society, what exactly is each one's sexuality and what it entails.
They are displaced, unplaced—products and victims and symp-
toms of the confused society—or nonsociety—of post–Civil War
America. Olive Chancellor is the most extreme case. Although
cultured and with a sense of her place in an élitist social coterie—
one could hardly call it "society" since no one seems quite to
know where that elusive entity is to be located—she is in a state of
serious psychological disarray. She is morbid, nervous, fixated on
her belief in "the great male conspiracy" and paranoid in her
sense that there is always some base masculine plot being aimed at
her (this paranoia is triggered by her anxiety that some man will

entice Verena Tarrant away). In every way she attempts to negate her own, and indeed female, sexuality. "There are women who are unmarried by accident, and others who are unmarried by option; but Olive Chancellor was unmarried by every implication of her being." And "She had absolutely no figure, and presented a certain appearance of feeling cold." I might mention here that in no other of his novels does James pay more attention to the physical appearance of his characters. For a writer who is supposed to shy away from the body he shows himself to be amazingly acute when it comes to registering the sheer corporeal presence of his characters, and what their bodies reveal about their relations to their own sexuality.

Olive speaks out of "outraged theory" and is "hungry for revenge." "She considered men in general as so much in the debt of the opposite sex that any individual woman had an unlimited credit with them; she could not possibly overdraw the general feminine account" (an attitude that is not uncommon in some feminist groups today). Among other things, this great novel has unexpected contemporary relevance. Ransom is right in his reply to Verena's claim that what Olive wants is "equal rights." " 'Oh, I thought what she wanted was simply a different inequality—simply to turn out the men altogether.' " In trying to force Verena to hate all men entirely and with her own twisted passion, Olive, inevitably, finally alienates her: "She felt Olive's grasp too clinching, too terrible." She perceives, correctly, that Olive's apparently idealistic dedication to the cause of feminism is gratingly unnatural, a psychic dissonance. "Olive's earnestness began to appear as inharmonious with the scheme of the universe as if it had been a broken saw." There is just one moment—it is an important one—when Olive seems momentarily to lapse from her virulent obsession and resentful aggression. They are listening to classical music in an elegant comfortable room—and the music is, briefly, therapeutic: "Civilisation, under such an influence, in such a setting, appeared to have done its work; harmony ruled the scene; human life ceased to be a battle. She went so far as to ask herself why one should quarrel with it; the relations of men and women, in that picturesque grouping, had not the air of being internecine." It is a glimpse of a possibility—a possible society—which is never realized in the book. It can only occur in a lapse, as it were. Shortly after the music ends, Olive's repressions and perversions are at work again—with a vengeance, we might say.

Basil Ransom is the opposition—in every way: a southern male, avowedly and ruthlessly reactionary. Some people have taken him to be the approved figure in the book—the firm, sensible, old-fashioned male rescuing Verena from a bunch of demented spinsters. This is to misread the book in a serious way. Basil Ransom is "very provincial," he operates from "narrow notions": his hero is Carlyle, preferably in his ranting denunciatory mode. He regards women as "essentially inferior to men, and infinitely tiresome when they declined to accept the lot which men had made for them." If Olive shows the bad affects of a Puritan culture, Basil has "the unregenerate imagination of the children of the cotton states." In other words, he grew up in a society based on slavery, and while he rejects the actual use of slaves, he carries over the notion of master/slave relationship into his attitude to women. He is not only a cynic, he is "aggressive and unmerciful," as Verena perceives. He may regard himself as the one sane man among a group of aberrant women, but he is himself—as Verena sees—perverse. He does have a strong sexual appeal, one to which Verena finally succumbs, but this is not a story of true love emerging at last. When he realizes that Verena is in love with him, under his spell, he is quite merciless. He literally takes possession of her—forcibly abducting her from the Music Hall in which she was to have given a great speech concerning the feminist cause. Verena is a much-handled girl—literally: from her wretched exploitative father who lays his hands on her head, ostensibly to put her into the kind of trance in which she could make her inspired speeches; on to the cold, suffocating, life-denying embrace of Olive; thence to the ruthless male hands of Basil who simply pulls her away with him by force. Verena is in every sense quite excessively manipulated.

One particular bit of male cruelty on the part of Basil should be noted. The finale of the book is set in the Music Hall where Verena is to give what is planned as a major speech. Her voice, we should note, is said to be particularly lovely. But Basil's thoughts run this way: "if he should become her husband he should know a way to strike her dumb." Olive is not wrong in saying to Verena that "it was because he knew that her voice had magic in it, and from the moment he caught its first note he had determined to destroy it. It was not tenderness that moved him—it was devilish malignity." Devilish or not, it is a purely repressive act, a crude assertion of power. He wants to privatize Verena, allow her no public life. The only platform she will have will be the dining-table. It is notable—and another sign of his very limited mind—that he finally feels he can urge marriage when one of his articles is accepted (most are rejected as being more suitable for the sixteenth century!) by a magazine with the distinctly unmemorable title of *Rational Review*. One can well imagine that their limited ideas and parochial stupidities could hardly be less than the extremist absurdities that he attacks in Olive. And if he thinks that is the basis for a secure career . . . then he is even more foolish than we thought. But the significance is that the male pen cancels the female voice: his writing is to replace, destroy, her speaking. In its most extreme implications it means that his phallus will negate her voice, deny her utterance, that organ, that gift, through which she articulates her self as a *self*—and thus disavow her full humanity. In a small way it is an act of pure sexual totalitarianism. James knew very well what he was doing—he always did—when he placed one of the first meetings between Basil and Verena in the Memorial Hall of Harvard, in which there is a chamber consecrated to those who died in the Civil War. That particular war is over, but the unending war between the sexes is entering a new phase. "Slavery" may have been abolished, but in this confused society slavery in various forms can be endlessly reinstituted. Basil Ransom, of course, has his attractive qualities, and the power of his deep appeal to Verena is made quite plausible. But as Verena goes away with—is pulled away by—him, she is in tears. "It is to be feared that with the union, so far from brilliant, into which she was about to enter, these were not the last she was destined to shed," thus James concludes the book, offering us the hint, as Irving Howe once put it, that "Ransom and Verena, married at last, would live unhappily ever after."

In all this Verena is the victim—herself asking little, nothing, but being continually exploited, appropriated. Her air is one of "artless enthusiasm, of personal purity." She is a "human gazelle" in a world of hunters and trappers. Olive's attempt to bind her is perhaps the most extreme—but only an extreme form of what others seek to do to her. "The fine web of authority, of dependence, that her strenuous companion had woven about her, was now as dense as a suit of golden mail." Such armor is a prison, not a defense, and is a cruelly incongruous encasement for the young, lithe, free-moving body of the pure Verena. The essence of Verena "was the extraordinary generosity with which she could expose herself, give herself away, turn herself inside out, for the satisfaction of a person who made demands of her." There is no other such generosity in the book: in a world of takers she is the one giver. She is thus not only a victim—all too easily exploited—she is an anomaly. She alone is in no way perverse, and in this she is totally alone; hence the aura of pathos around this gay, artless, pure young figure. Her generosity is her doom. That such should be the case is a profound indictment of the society into which she was born. The book on the whole is written in a spirit of incisive satiric humor—among other things it is simply one of James's funniest books. But the humor bites and the issues revealed are deeply serious ones. And the fate that gathers round Verena finally gives the book a somber tone.

The novel is rich in secondary characters—both female and male—and in all of them there is some "perversity"—some falling away from, or failure to achieve, any kind of full sexual humanity. The veteran champion of New England causes, Miss Birdseye, is drawn with much sympathy as well as sustained, gentle mockery (her "charity began at home and ended nowhere"). What she shares with other supporters of the feminist cause is a rather pathetic loss of feature and form—as though dedication to the cause has contributed to a loss of sexually differentiating outlines. "The long practice of philanthropy had not given accent to her features; it had rubbed out their transitions, their meanings." Generous, kind, vague, tired, and ineffectual, "this essentially formless old woman, who had no more outline than a bundle of hay" seems to have sacrificed her actual female body and identity to the female cause. It is a mark of the encompassing humanity of James's art that he makes the account of her death—a gentle, final fading away—genuinely poignant. Different in character is the more energetic and redoubtably dedicated Dr. Prance. Unsentimental and uninterested in the too abstract matter of "rights," she unswervingly and impersonally concentrates exclusively on her study of health and the body. But it is the generic body—again, sexually undifferentiated. As she revealingly asserts, " 'Men and women are all the same to me. . . . *I don't see any difference*' " (my italics). She is at once sympathetic and somewhat inhuman. James makes the point comically rather than cruelly: "if she had been a boy she would have borne some relation to a girl, whereas Doctor Prance appeared to bear none whatever. Except her intelligent eye, she had no features to speak of." Whereas these and other feminists seem to suffer from this kind of radical effacement or obliteration of the female form—if not all distinguishing "features"—a woman like Mrs. Luna (Olive's sister and opposite) merely exploits her form and features in an exaggerated, if conventional way, in attempts to secure a husband. In her concern with dress, cosmetics, and adornments, and in her attempts to assume what she takes to be a beguiling "feminine" manner, she stereotypicalizes herself and is as much of a pathetic parody of the truly "female" as the committed feminists—if not more so.

If anything, some of the men are worse—and here one recurrent dehumanizing feature is of particular interest, since it involves a displacement of an authentic awareness of the body into an obsession with "print." The deceptively gentle and apparently obsequious and soft-mannered journalist, Mr. Pardon, would literally translate—transform—everything and everyone into print. "For this ingenuous son of his age all *distinction* between the person and the artist has ceased to exist. . . . everything and everyone were everybody's business. All things with him referred themselves to print, and print meant simply infinite reporting. . . . He regarded the mission of mankind upon earth as a perpetual evolution of telegrams; *everything to him was very much the same . . .*" (my italics). Again, there is a loss of "distinction" and all sense of "difference," sexual and indeed human. An even more extreme case is the unctuous, repellent charlatan, Dr. Tarrant (Verena's father). He spends all his spare time hanging around newspaper printing rooms. "He was always trying to find out what was 'going in'; he would have liked to go in himself, bodily. . . ." One could hardly have it rendered more specifically: the man would literally like to transform his body into print. This is even more "perverse" than the feminists' tendency to disincarnate themselves into lectures. But both reveal varying degrees of a prevailing tendency or compulsion to attempt to transform the self into public-ity—the printed word, the platform voice. The possible fulfillments of the private life, the achievable pleasures of the appropriate integration of body and voice, the authentic satisfaction of some degree of full human communication, are rarely envisioned in this novel—where they are not positively disdained or denied.

A final word should just take note of the various city settings, social occasions, and landscapes that James deploys so skillfully in the book: Boston, already showing signs of dirt and pollution resulting from industrialization; evocations of the ambiguous ruins of the postwar South; the confusions and precariousness of life in contemporary New York; the protected parochialism and cosseted "culture" of Harvard (overbearing mothers and amiable shallow sons); the decaying shipbuilding yards of Marion on Cape Cod, where the atmosphere of mouldering decline not only provides a suitable setting for the climax of the book but also reminds us of a past era and a lost greatness in American history. All these contribute to that "density of specification" that James thought a novel should have. However we wish to define the social novel, on the general grounds of conveying a sense of the moral and physical condition (or malaise) of a society in a distinct historical and geographical setting, *The Bostonians* is the finest one James ever wrote.

### III

When James turned to his second attempt at a major social naturalist novel, he shifted his attention from a reform movement to a revolutionary one, from the feminists of Boston to a somewhat vague socialist-anarchist-revolutionary group in London. The year the book was written and published, 1886, saw the Trafalgar Square riots in London and the Haymarket killings in Chicago—revolution in an unorganized, uncoordinated, threatening sense was distinctly in the air, and it was an astute choice on James's part to attempt a major novel dealing with this menacing feeling of a threat to society coming from the lower classes. James was not a very precise sociologist any more than he was a particularly factually well-informed historian—he worked through a sense of the past, his genius for registering the total atmosphere of a place and all that was latent or impregnated in it. Thus in *The Princess Casamassima* the politics of the revolutionary group are various, inconsistent, and vague. This was not only a shrewd choice on James's part—by inclination he was not especially knowledgeable about revolutionary politics or cells, conspiracies, underground groups, and such—but it is also a deliberate tactic. The vagueness of the politics was reflected in the vagueness of the threat, and it is just this sense of some possible imminent but as yet indefinable social upheaval that James manages to convey. Temperamentally, as I said, James was hardly in much sympathy with this part of his subject. Not that he had any illusions about the injustices and degradations of the English class system. At this time he wrote of the English upper class: "The condition of that body seems to me in many ways to be the same rotten and collapsible one as that of the French aristocracy before the revolution—minus cleverness and conversation; or perhaps it is more like the heavy, congested and depraved Roman world upon which the barbarians came down. In England the Huns and Vandals will have to come up—from the black depths of the (in the people) enormous misery. . . ." Among the many things that James was inhaling in his beloved London was the vast amount of human suffering it contained. There are many passages in the novel referring to it: for example, "the season was terribly hard; and as in that lower world one walked with one's ear nearer the ground the deep perpetual groan of London misery seemed to swell and swell and form the whole undertone of life." And he undoubtedly did feel that "the people was only a sleeping lion, already breathing shorter and beginning to stretch its limbs and stiffen its claws." But, for all that, James the artist could not really get inside a political movement, nor really explore in Zolaesque detail the actual conditions of urban squalor and misery. So, while the book pays notional respect to the revolutionaries and their cause, its real sympathies go in the opposite direction—as a brief look at the main characters and the plot will indicate.

As his hero or central figure, James chose not a robust child of the working people but an anomaly. Hyacinth Robinson (one can hardly imagine someone called "Hyacinth" working passionately alongside a Lenin!) is the illegitimate son of a decadent English lord who was murdered by a working-class French prostitute. Thus, perhaps rather too obviously, there is a clear genetic reason for the duality in his nature. From the mother comes a sense of resentment at the exploitative decadence of the upper classes;

from the father, an innate tendency toward gentility and an inas-
suageable appetite for the elegancies of high society and aesthetic
satisfactions of great art. A visit to his dying mother in prison
sows in the boy's mind "the seeds of shame and rancour," it
makes him "conscious of his stigma, of his exquisite vulnerabil-
ity." Both as a product and a person he really fits in nowhere, nor
does he—can he—really know who, what he really is. In his
person he is small, not strong, but obviously a "gentleman,"
very delicate, and with "something jaunty and romantic, almost
theatrical, in his whole little person." Physically he is a rather
amusing incongruity when seen alongside the strapping London
lass Millicent, who is one of his lady friends. A true relationship
between them is inconceivable, and indeed they finally move
apart. He also looks foreign, out-of-place. When Millicent suggests that he could get a place in the theater—"he was on the point
of replying that he didn't care for fancy costumes, he wished to go
through life in his own character; but he checked himself with the
reflexion that this was exactly what he was apparently destined
not to do. His own character? He was to cover that up as carefully
as possible; he was to go through life in a mask, in a borrowed
mantle; he was to be every day and every hour an actor."

James was to take up the problematical relation between acting
and life in his next novel, but here we can notice one important
result of Hyacinth's dubiety about his own self. Given his social—
not to say ontological—insecurity, he is easily influenced, led
in different directions, seduced into a particular group or by a
stronger person, like the revolutionary Paul Muniment. In this he
resembles Verena Tarrant who was also a lonely anomaly in her
own society, easily taken over and influenced by other people.
And just as Verena never really takes to the cause of feminist reform with the ardent convictions and obsessions of Olive and the
others, neither does Hyacinth really take on the revolutionary
cause with the passion of a genuine radical. He gives his word—
which is to have important repercussions—but not his heart.
They are two of James's typical characters—Hyacinth is "one of
the disinherited, one of the expropriated, one of the exceptionally
interesting," and so in her different way is Verena. These and
many other comparable figures are near to James's heart—and he
himself was displaced from America to Europe, and in a subtler
sense from life to art. There are moments when Hyacinth does

regret social wrongs, and indeed in joining the secret political group and giving his word that he will do whatever deed is asked of him, he is effectively giving his life to the revolutionary cause. But what he really wants is initiation into the life of real society and art. Even his profession—bookbinding—is not typical of the generic working-class figure, and when he does gain some access to aristocratic life, it is not resentment or a desire for revenge that he feels, but only the sad extent of his own "exclusion." His indictment of society comes more from what he has seen and experienced of deprivation and privilege than from any genuine ideology—and it can move him to real eloquence:

> People come and go, and buy and sell, and drink and dance, and make money and make love, and seem to know nothing and suspect nothing and think of nothing; and iniquities flourish, and the misery of half the world is prated about as a "necessary evil," and generations rot away and starve in the midst of it, and day follows day, and everything is for the best in the best of possible worlds. All that's one half of it; the other half is that everything's doomed! In silence, in darkness, but under the feet of each one of us, the revolution lives and works. It's a wonderful, immeasurable trap, on the lid of which society performs its antics.

Hyacinth's tantalizing and disturbing contacts with the fine amenities of upper-class life come about through the mysterious woman after whom the book is named. Christina Light was the enigmatic and destructive woman in *Roderick Hudson*, and she reappears in this book, married to but separated from Prince Casamassima, to be as fatal a torment for Hyacinth as she was for Roderick. Her appearance stretches plausibility a little, but her behavior does not. She is a rich bored woman who has had everything and all the lovers she wants, and is always on the lookout for some new excitement and distraction. In her ennui she has turned to flirting with revolutionaries, as if they could give her a taste of the real life that her jaded senses no longer find in other society. Today we would call her attitude radical chic. Her companion, Madame Grandoni, calls her a *capricciosa*, and warns Hyacinth not to give himself up to her. Paul Muniment calls her a monster but seems to be taking up with her after she drops Hyacinth, as she does near the end of the book. She first takes up

Hyacinth in a theater—always a significant venue in James—and it is she who gives him a glimpse of the graces and seductions and finesses of upper-class social life, particularly at her country house, Medley. Hyacinth's visit there is a vision of earthly delights, an intoxication from which he scarcely recovers. That he is capable of being devoted to the princess is clear. That for her he is just the satisfaction of another whim is also clear. "Why shouldn't I have my bookbinder after all? In attendance, you know—it would be awfully *chic*. We might have immense fun. . . ." Artists, bookbinders, Italian princes, revolutionaries . . . all immense fun—for a time. Hyacinth succumbs to the atmosphere around her, but he also succumbs to his experience of the world. And she can see the pathos in his position: " 'to be constituted as you're constituted, to be conscious of the capacity you must feel, and yet to look at the good things of life only through the glass of the pastry-cook's window!' "

Some of those good things Hyacinth sees on his first visit to Europe. In Paris, while well aware of the French Revolution, "what was most present to him was not its turpitude and horror, but its magnificent energy, the spirit of creation that had been in it, not the spirit of destruction." His shift of allegiance from politics to art is all but complete. Paris gives him "a sense of everything that might hold one to the world, of the sweetness of not dying, the fascination of great cities, the charm of travel and discovery, the generosity of admiration." These are not the sentiments of a burning radical. But having achieved this vision, Hyacinth cannot live it out, or put it into practice, or do anything with it, or about it, whatever. For one thing "there was no peace for him between the two currents that flowed in his nature, the blood of his passionate, plebeian mother and that of his long-descended super-civilized sire. They continued to toss him from one side to the other; they arrayed him in intolerable defiances and revenges against himself." For another, he is ordered to carry out his pledge and assassinate a certain duke—a task hardly in line with his temperament. Then again, while it is inconceivable that he should sustain a relationship with that daughter of London, Millicent, it is also only too evident that the princess will play with him and then drop him. And while he can never be at home in his own class, he can never hope to gain lasting access to one above him. He has no one. He has nowhere to go—indeed, nowhere to *be*. It is a fitting end to the novel that he should be found dead, having used the gun given to him to kill the duke to commit suicide. This sad conclusion dramatizes a problem that becomes prominent in James's work. A person may achieve a certain refinement and subtlety of sensibility that will simply make it impossible for him or her to operate in any of the given social or nonsocial spaces of the world. There are extreme solutions—the bullet in the head, the retreat into art; both, in very different ways, involve some kind of loss of participation in life, though, to be sure, writing is more creative than suicide. But James was to go on wondering whether there were any other solutions—besides the bullet and the pen.

## IV

Both *The Bostonians* and *The Princess Casamassima* were failures with the public. To William Dean Howells, James wrote in 1888 "I have entered upon evil days, I am still staggering a good deal under the mysterious and (to me) inexplicable damage wrought—apparently—upon my situation by my last novels." So he decided to abandon the type of large public themes he had been attempting, one reason being, as he said, his "sense of knowing terribly little about the kind of life I have attempted to describe." True of *The Princess Casamassima*, not true of *The Bostonians*. But it could also be that he had not only exhausted the themes of the naturalist social novel, he had also exhausted its form. He was to concentrate more and more on the small group, the individual, and embark on new fictional modes, but not before completing one more novel, which ranges widely enough to be characterized as one of his social novels of this period. That was *The Tragic Muse* in which he brought together the worlds—and claims—of politics, art, and theater in a rather unusual way. It was intended to be his final long novel: "*The Tragic Muse* is to be my last long novel," he wrote to his brother, so it is not surprising that he should take as his theme the whole problem of the relation of the artist to society, and to focus on the theater, the arena that he intended to enter to repair his fortunes. James saw his theme as "some dramatic picture of the 'artist-life' and of the difficult terms on which it is at the best secured and enjoyed, the general question of its having to be not altogether paid for. To 'do something about art'—*art, that is, as a human complication and a social stumbling block*—must have been for me early a good deal of a nursed intention, the conflict between art and 'the world' striking me thus betimes as one of the half-dozen great primary motives" (my italics). The words in italics do indeed sum up a theme that generated a large number of stories and novellas by James and, in this case, a whole novel. Put at its simplest, the problem was the relationship between the artist and marriage or sexuality (the "human complication"), and between the artist and society (art as "a social stumbling block")—the problem in each case being whether to renounce or participate. James himself renounced marriage and, apart from a very late flowering of a tolerably well-controlled homoeroticism, sex; he participated in society but was mentally—artistically—detached from it. All his libidinal energy seems to have gone into the eye—and the pen. But note that even James, so supremely urbane, sees a *conflict* between art and society. Not that he was thinking of art as being deliberately subversive as, say, Sartre might. But simply, to the extent that one was an artist, one was so much less a social being, even a citizen—even, at times, a human being. And yet, for James, art was the supreme value in life: indeed, in the final analysis it gave value to life. It is hardly surprising that the conflict between art and the world struck him as "one of the half-dozen great primary motives." In his own case it was *the* primary one.

The novel is long and at times complicated, yet the organizing structure is almost diagrammatically clear. Nick Dormer (son of a great politician) is effectively offered a safe seat in the House of Commons, plus a high social position, if he marries an eminently political-social lady, Julia Dallow. But, under the influence of a rather curious spokesman for art, Gabriel Nash, he turns down that life and takes up painting. At the end he has painted Julia Dallow's portrait and it is an open question whether they will not, after all, finally marry and—who knows, the not notably successful painter Nick Dormer might once again turn to politics. The other relationship, running concurrently with Nick's fluctuations between Julia/politics and painting, is between Peter Sherringham and Miriam Rooth. He is a successful diplomat and she is a young actress who rapidly achieves fame. Peter is in love with her and offers to marry her, if she will give up the stage (shades of Basil Ransom!). In his attempt to persuade her, he says, " 'The stage is great, no doubt, but the world is greater. It's a bigger theatre than any of those places in the Strand. We'll go in for realities instead of fables, and you'll do them far better than you do the fables.' " She is not persuaded, but we may note that the problem of just what is reality and what is fable, and how one can with any confidence draw the line between them, is very much a part of this book. Peter, somewhat perversely, asks Miriam if she would let him sacrifice his work and career and prospects to join her in the world of the theater and " 'simply become your appendage?' " But Miriam is a quicker and more powerful woman than Verena Tarrant, and she unanswerably replies: " 'My dear fellow, you invite me with the best conscience in the world to become yours.' " As it transpires, Miriam marries one of her theatrical assistants, Basil Dashwood, and Peter marries the socially correct Biddy Dormer. They are true to their respective worlds.

Such is the story, and one can readily see how these relationships allow for long debates about politics and painting; social office and theater; public service and private dedications—and it is the debates that really constitute the interest of the book, because in a crucial way the book is let down by its two main men. Nick Dormer is first singled out by "the wandering blankness that sat at moments in his eyes, as if he had no attention at all," and James must have named him deliberately with the French word for sleep (*dormir*) in mind, for a very sleepy individual he is, marked more by vacancies than saliences as he drifts somewhat somnambulistically through the novel. He is not convincing as a politician, as a painter, or as a lover; not, that is, as a man. Peter is a public service type all right, but his sudden wild passion for Miriam (although we know that, of course, that sort of thing can happen to anyone) is somewhat implausible. He is not much less sleepy than Nick, despite all his avowed ambition. They both seem somehow to live life with their hands in their pockets—more given to a kind of elegant indolence than intensities of infatuation. No, the saving interest of the book is the woman, the actress, the tragic muse, Miriam Rooth. This is because in his study of her James managed to say a number of things about the problems of what exactly constitutes a self, a character, a subject, an identity, which were a good deal ahead of his time, though now well recognized. But if they are now so recognized, it is because of the kind of pioneering psychological work that writers like James did toward the end of the last century.

Miriam is half-Jewish, a wanderer over continents, a "vagabond." She is by nature displaced in and from society, just as Julia Dallow incorporates the very ideal of social place and mastered hierarchy. The problem for Peter, for James, for us, is, What is *in* her; what, who is she? Really. Her face at times seems a "persistent vacancy" and she herself is thoroughly "plastic." "Miriam was a beautiful, active, fictive, impossible young woman, of a past age and undiscoverable country. . . ." But still, what is she? Here is a key passage summarizing Peter's thoughts:

> It came over him suddenly that so far from there being any question of her having the histrionic nature, she simply had it in such perfection that she was always acting; that her existence was a series of parts assumed for the moment, each changed for the next, before the perpetual mirror of some curiosity or admiration or wonder—some spectatorship that she perceived or imagined in the people about her . . . [she was a woman] whose identity resided in the continuity of her personations, so that she had no moral privacy, as he phrased it to himself, but lived in a high wind of exhibition, of figuration—such a woman was a kind of monster, in whom of necessity there would be nothing to like, because there would be nothing to take hold of.

He tells her she has " 'no nature of [her] own,' " that her " 'only feeling is a feigned one,' " that she has no character—or a hundred. "She delighted in novels, poems, perversions, misrepresentations and evasions, and had a capacity for smooth, superfluous falsification which made Sherringham think her sometimes an amusing and sometimes a tedious inventor." But she is more than that. She is a great actress with the endless recession of irresolvable ambiguities that that implies, and the unanswerable questions it raises. Because where does acting stop? Not at the door of the theater. What about the House of Commons? What about the great formal social occasions Julia Dallow loves to organize and promote? Miriam is said to be a "mountebank" (a common word in the book) associated with "mountebanks and mimes" but who exactly is, and is not, a "mountebank"? Are there none in politics, in high society?

To ask the question is to realize not that much of theater may be based on everyday life, but that everyday life is simply a series of different kinds of theaters. What is a performance but "an instinct put in its place," and if "all reflection is affectation, and all acting is reflection"—well then, where exactly are we? Acting indicates "the communicableness of style" (another recurring word) and which part of society does not have its style, its styles? To look at Miriam's face is to look at a "mobile mask," she herself "a series of masks." But perhaps the real face is to be found in the mask—and perhaps we are most ourselves when we are "playing." At another time Peter feels, "her character was simply to hold you by the particular spell; any other—the good-nature of home, the relation to her mother, her friends, her lovers, her debts, the practice of virtues or industries or vices—was not worth speaking of. These things were the fiction and shadows; *the representation was the deep substance*" (my italics). This is not mere playing with paradox. James is probing very deeply into our too unexamined assumptions about the priorities of reality that put our relational life above our representational life. An ontological shift of some considerable importance is going on here. And if the Miriam Rooth offstage is a mercurial unreliable, perhaps even promiscuous person, the truth of her own statement remains: " 'One may live in paint and tinsel, but one isn't absolutely without a soul.' " One may have as much of a soul as a politician or a society hostess—perhaps more, for they are often deceived, self-mystified, by the paint and tinsel *they* live in, live *on*; Miriam is not. She has fewer deceptions about herself than anyone in the book. She may like "superfluous falsifications," yet in the deepest sense she doesn't lie. She is, in truth, a remarkable figure of worryingly ambiguous truth, and certainly the most "awake" character in the book.

A word must be said about the strange figure of Gabriel Nash. Critics have speculated as to whether he was based on Oscar Wilde or some other contemporary aesthete; it hardly matters. Others have seen him as James's symbol of "the spirit of art," which is certainly too simple. He is a drifting, fleeting, transient presence, speaking always for art, for feeling, for being—but never for doing. Some of James's own ideas and opinions are clearly discernible in Nash's utterances, but that does not mean he is not a figure to be regarded with a certain amount of irony. Here are a few of his sayings: " 'Shades of impression, of appreciation. . . . My only behaviour is my feelings. . . . I accomplish my happiness—it seems to me that's something. I have feelings, I have sensations: let me tell you that's not so common. . . . To be what one *may* be, really and efficaciously . . . to feel it and understand it, to accept, adopt it, embrace it—that's conduct, that's life.' " This was not conduct as Matthew Arnold understood it, to be sure, since Nash's notion of conduct seems to exclude any kind of commitment to relationships, to any kind of work, to any society—to anything at all. He is a perpetual tourist, a floater—very light indeed, and so his benign words seem also light, with no substance, no substantial experience behind them. His facile aphorisms are devoid of context or application. It is entirely appropriate that at the end of the novel, in a rather Emersonian or Whitmanish way, he simply dissolves: "Nash has melted back into the elements—he is part of the ambient air." The person who remains most real in all her mastery of corporeal falsifications and representations is of course the tragic muse herself. James chose his title well. (Note that the titles of all three of these "social" novels refer to women and never to men. James knew what he knew best.)

## V

The novel was not a great failure, but James had decided that he had to try something else. To his brother he wrote: "I shall never make my fortune—nor anything like it, but—I know what I shall do and it won't be bad." As F. W. Dupee once remarked, it was a curious thing to say. Because what James was about to do was to attempt, exactly—unscrupulously—to make his fortune in the theater. And what he did there was "pretty bad." I propose to say nothing about the plays, not because they are *so* irremediably bad, but because they are not, somehow, of the essence of James. He was trying to falsify his art to make money, and while there is nothing immoral in that, the result in James's case was a series of productions of art somehow not quite his own. Clearly he learned a lot from these years of theatrical writing. He was always brilliant at dialogue, but after writing for the theater—in which, apart from scenery and bodily gesture, everything must be revealed in speech—he became an absolute master, and indeed later wrote one of his most brilliant novels (*The Awkward Age*) almost entirely in dialogue. But he learned another lesson. One of the great powers of his art was the originality of his metaphors, often developed at great length, usually to depict elusive or crucial inner dramas or thought processes. It is just those metaphors and those accounts of inner movements that cannot be translated onto the stage. When James returned to novel writing he knew more about his own essential powers, so that his last novels are as rich in metaphor as they are in dialogue. But while avoiding the plays, I want to find space to mention two other aspects of James's work that might be overlooked in a short survey. First of all—he was a superb travel writer. He could register the sense of a place incomparably, working not through information but impressions, at times seemingly as able to communicate with—listen to—buildings and scenes, as with people; at times, more able. I will simply give three examples, drawn from his three main travel works (a fourth, *The American Scene*, will be discussed in the next chapter)—temporarily abandoning chronology. First this, from *Italian Hours* (1909) concerning Venice, for James the most magical of cities:

> It is a city in which, I suspect, there is very little strenuous thinking, and yet it is a city in which there must be as much happiness as misery. . . . The Venetian people have little to call their own—little more than the bare privilege of leading their lives in the most beautiful of towns. Their habitations are decayed; their taxes heavy; their pockets light; their opportunities few. One receives an impression, however, that life presents itself to them with attractions not accounted for in this meagre train of advantages, and that they are on better terms with it than many people who have made a better bargain. They lie in the sunshine; they dabble in the sea; they wear bright rags; they fall into attitudes and harmonies; they assist at an eternal *conversazione*. It is not easy to say that one would have them other than they are, and it certainly would make an immense difference should they be better fed. The number of persons in Venice who evidently never have enough to eat is painfully

large; but it would be more painful if we did not equally perceive that the rich Venetian temperament may bloom upon a
dog's allowance. Nature has been kind to it, and sunshine and
leisure and conversation and beautiful views form the greater
part of its sustenance. It takes a great deal to make a successful
American, but to make a happy Venetian it takes only a hand-
ful of quick sensibility. . . . Not their misery, doubtless, but the
way they elude their misery, is what pleases the sentimental
tourist, who is gratified by the sight of a beautiful race that lives
by the aid of its imagination.

And then this, the concluding paragraph of *A Little Tour in
France* (1884), since it catches James in such a characteristic pos-
ture and mood:

I think the thing that pleased me best at Dijon was the little old
Parc, a charming public garden, about a mile from the town, to
which I walked by a long, straight autumnal avenue. It is a
*jardin français* of the last century—a dear old place, with little
blue-green perspectives and alleys and *rondpoints*, in which
everything balances. I went there late in the afternoon, without
meeting a creature, though I had hopes I should meet the Prési-
dent de Brosses. At the end of it was a little river that looked
like a canal, and on the further bank was an old-fashioned villa,
close to the water, with a little French garden of its own. On the
hither side was a bench, on which I seated myself, lingering
a good while; for this was just the sort of place I like. It was the
furthermost point of my little tour. I thought that over, as I sat
there, on the eve of taking the express to Paris; and as the light
faded in the Parc the vision of some of the things I had seen
became more distinct.

And finally, from *English Hours* (1905), part of his evocation of
Rye, the place which he was to choose as his home for his final
years:

I seem to myself to have lain on the grass somewhere, as a boy,
poring over an English novel of the period, presumably quite
bad—for they were pretty bad then too—and losing myself in
the idea of just such another scene as this. But even could I re-
discover the novel I wouldn't go back to it. It couldn't have
been as good as this; for this—all concrete and doomed and

minimised as it is—is the real thing. The other little gardens, other little odds and ends of crooked brown wall and supported terrace and glazed winter sun-trap, lean over the cliff that still, after centuries, keeps its rude drop; they have beneath them the river, a tide that comes and goes, and the mile or more of grudging desert level, beyond it, which now throw the sea to the near horizon, where, on summer days, with a depth of blue and a scattered gleam of sail, it looks forgiving and resigned. The little old shipyards at the base of the rock are for the most part quite empty, with only vague piles of brown timber and the deposit of generations of chips; yet a fishing boat or two are still on the stocks—an "output" of three or four a year!—and the ring of the hammer on the wood, a sound, in such places, rare to the contemporary ear, comes up, through the sunny stillness, to your meditative perch.

The other genre in which James also excelled was the field of criticism and critical theory. He wrote many important articles on contemporary writers, such as George Eliot, Emerson, Turgenev, Flaubert, Trollope, etc. (see, for example, *Partial Portraits*, 1888). He also wrote theater criticism and art criticism (as in, for example, *Picture and Text*, 1893). But most important, he raised the thinking about the art of fiction to a new level of self-consciousness and sophistication. His essay "The Art of Fiction," published in 1884, is not only a crucial statement by James about his own art, as he saw it. It marks a turning point in the history of the theory of the novel. I shall run together some of the key statements from this extremely important document.

It goes without saying that you will not write a good novel unless you possess the sense of reality; but it will be difficult to give you a recipe for calling that sense into being. Humanity is immense, and reality has a myriad forms; the most one can affirm is that some of the flowers of fiction have the odor of it, and others have not. . . . Experience is never limited, and it is never complete; it is an immense sensibility, a kind of huge spider-web of the finest silken threads suspended in the chamber of consciousness,[1] and catching every air-borne parti-

---

1. Henry James's lifelong fascination with "the chamber of consciousness" corresponds in many ways to his brother William's psychological and scientific interest in the "stream of consciousness."

cle in its tissue.[2] It is the very atmosphere of the mind; and when the mind is imaginative—much more when it happens to be that of a man of genius—it takes to itself the faintest hints of life, it converts the very pulses of the air into revelations. . . . The power to guess the unseen from the seen, to trace the implication of things, to judge the whole piece by the pattern, the condition of feeling life in general so completely that you are well on your way to knowing any particular corner—this cluster of gifts may almost be said to constitute experience . . . if experience consists of impressions, it may be said that impressions *are* experience, just as (have we not seen it?) they are the very air we breathe. . . . One can speak best from one's own taste, and I may therefore venture to say that the air of reality (solidity of specification) seems to me the supreme virtue of a novel—the merit on which all its other merits (including that conscious moral purpose of which Mr. Besant speaks) helplessly and submissively depend. . . . A novel is a living thing, all one and continuous, like any other organism, and in proportion as it lives will it be found, I think, that in each of the parts there is something of each of the other parts. . . . What is character but the determination of incident? What is incident but the illustration of character? What is either a picture or a novel that is *not* of character? . . . A psychological reason is, to my imagination, an object adorably pictorial; to catch the tint of its complexion—I feel as if that idea might inspire one to Titianesque efforts. There are few things more exciting to me, in short, than a psychological reason, and yet, I protest, the novel seems to me the most magnificent form of art . . . the deepest quality of a work of art will always be the quality of the mind of the producer. In proportion as that intelligence is fine will the novel, the picture, the statue partake of the substance of beauty and truth. To be constituted of such elements is, to my mind, to have purpose enough. No good novel will ever proceed from a superficial mind; that seems to me an axiom which for the artist in fiction, will cover all needful moral

2. The image of the web has become so well known that it is perhaps worth noting that a similar use had appeared in Walter Pater's *The Renaissance* (1873), which James must have known. Pater writes of consciousness as that "magic web . . . woven through and through us . . . penetrating us with a network, subtler than our subtlest nerves yet bearing in it the central forces of the world" (from the chapter on "Winckelmann").

ground. . . . Remember that your first duty is to be as complete as possible—to make as perfect a work. Be generous and delicate and pursue the prize.

With Henry James, English writing about the theory of the novel comes of age.

## VI

Many of James's more remarkable works of fiction during this period emerged as short stories or novellas—indeed we will have only one other clearly major "novel" to refer to. *The Reverberator* (1888), for instance, was for James a short *"jeu d'esprit."* The tone is indeed light, and the story a slight romantic one. Yet it touched on a topic of real importance—the growing power of the American New Journalism. As early as 1838 James Fenimore Cooper had inveighed against the power of the press in *The American Democrat*: "when the number of prints is remembered, and the avidity with which they are read is brought into the account, we are made to perceive that the entire nation, in a moral sense, breathes an atmosphere of falsehoods. . . . If newspapers are useful in overthrowing tyrants, it is only to establish a tyranny of their own. . . . As the press of this country now exists, it would seem to be expressly devised by the great agent of mischief, to depress and destroy all that is good, and to elevate and advance all that is evil in the nation." Matters had got a good deal worse by James's day, and he had already made some tart, satiric observations on the American press in *The Bostonians*, where the charlatan Selah Tarrant reveres newspapers above all phenomena ("Human existence to him, indeed, was a huge publicity"), and the somewhat odious Matthias Pardon is shown to hold the same perverted opinion ("everything and everyone were everyone's business. All things, with him, referred themselves to print, and print simply meant infinite reporting. . . . He regarded the mission of mankind upon earth as a perpetual evolution of telegrams"). James could be amused and amusing about this phenomenon, but he could see also its dire side and implications: there were two actual incidents concerning betrayed privacy and intimacies that took place shortly before he started on *The Reverberator* and he outlined a definite intention to attack the baleful influence of the press, to take on "a type of newspaper man, a man whose ideal is the energetic reporter. I should like to *bafouer* the vulgarity and hideousness of this, the impudent invasion of privacy, the extinction of all conception of privacy, etc." The result was George Flack and his newspaper—*The Reverberator*.

The story itself is fairly simple. Francie Dosson, the daughter of one of those peripatetic American families in Europe about whom James wrote so often, falls in love with a Frenchified American, Gaston Probert. He is an American who has never seen America and whose family has become deeply involved in the highest French aristocracy. In getting engaged to the somewhat naïve and uncultured Francie, Gaston has to use various strategies to make her acceptable to his family. He succeeds. But then Francie—in her innocence (or colossal lack of circumspection)—tells all she knows about this élite Franco-American family to the young American, George Flack, who had originally courted her. He publishes everything she tells him in a highly scandalous article in *The Reverberator*, and Gaston's family is duly appalled, horrified, and mortified. Francie does not excuse herself—" 'I am only an American girl' " she says with fetching simplicity, and Gaston has to decide whether to let her go or risk being "cut" by his family if he marries her. He finally decides on the latter—it is clearly a matter of his own salvation that he should emerge into independence and break out of his mindless and slavish servitude to his family. So the ending is happy enough, though it is not clear where they are all going.

But James's main focus is on George Flack, about whom he is devastatingly funny: "He was not a particular person, but a sample or memento—reminding one of certain 'goods' for which there is a steady popular demand. You would scarcely have expected him to have a name other than that of his class: a number, like that of the day's newspaper, would have been the most that you would count on, and you would have expected vaguely to find the number high—somewhere up in the millions." Flack's contention is that the "private" life is over. " 'That's about played out, any way, the idea of sticking up a sign of 'private' and thinking you can keep the place to yourself. You can't do it—you can't keep out the light of the Press.' " After her mistake in transmitting family confidences to him, and then seeing the shattering effect it has, Francie thinks "of the lively and chatty letters that they had always seen in the papers and wondered whether they *all* meant a violation of sanctities, a convulsion of homes, a burning of smitten faces, a rupture of girls' engagements." The answer is—all too often, yes. James certainly is somewhat ironic about the extreme reaction of the Proberts to the violation of their somewhat too preciously cherished sanctities. But the danger of the George Flacks of the world and all they stood for, was real enough to him. And almost in passing, James touches on a problem that becomes central to his work. Francie and the Dossons simply take people "at their word," and this makes Gaston Probert realize something: "They had not in the least seen what was manner, the minimum of decent profession, and what the subtle resignation of old races who have known a long historical discipline and have conventional forms for their feelings—*forms resembling singularly little the feelings themselves*" (my italics). An extension of this problem concerns the fate of "sincerity" in a society that employs a high code of "compliment"—which is at bottom an empty code: "with such a high standard of compliment where after all was sincerity? And without sincerity how could people get on together when it came to their settling down to common life?" Large and serious questions, which James could hardly engage with deeply if he was not to damage and complicate the texture of this light comedy. But elsewhere he would ask them again. And again.

*The Aspern Papers* (1888) has come to be recognized as one of James's most remarkable pieces of work. It is a substantial novella, recounted by an unnamed narrator, and it is quite extraordinarily rich and subtle, with a stringent mixture of high comedy and telling pathos. The narrator is a critic, an editor, and he is convinced that some precious papers of his adored poet—Jeffrey Aspern (Byron was probably in mind)—are still in the possession of Aspern's mistress who, incredibly enough, is still alive in Venice. So to Venice he goes, prepared to stop at virtually nothing to gain possession of the putative papers. What he does stop at is the distinctly moving climax of the story. As the story is narrated in the first-person, we have to work out how to take the narrator, what to make of him, morally speaking, how to assess his own rationalizations, justifications, self-exonerations (a device perfected by Browning in his monologues, which James certainly knew well)—so the story offers a particular exercise in the problematics of reading. The narrator seems honest enough about his lack of scruple: " 'Hypocrisy, duplicity are my only chance.' " He knows the old lady—Juliana Bordereau—hates any kind of inquiry or publicity, so he has to find a way to insinuate himself into her house. He does this oddly—and comically—by presenting himself at the house and begging to rent rooms there in the old palazzo because it has a garden, and he simply must have a garden. This garden, incidentally, with all its iconographic associations, adds significantly to the incredibly rich and suggestive atmosphere of the story. It is a "garden in the middle of the sea," with the crumbling evocative architecture of the old palazzo, of old Venice, all around it. What takes place in this setting of meeting and mingling elements is a drama concerning how the present—in one way—seeks to appropriate the past. Precious things—great loves, great buildings, great poets, great papers— are always vanishing: there is a great deal here of "the poetry of the thing outlived and lost and gone." The narrator as critic justifies his salvage operation, as it were, as in this exchange with Juliana:

> "Do you think it's right to rake up the past?"
> "I don't know that I know what you mean by raking it up; but how can we get at it unless we dig a little? The present has such a rough way of treading it down."

Now we know why he insisted on having a garden. In its adjacency to the house it serves as a metonymic substitute for the real focus of his desire; for it is in the palazzo that he most wants to "rake up" and "dig a little"—for the dead papers rather than for the living flowers.

Of course he has a point, and the present has, in some way, to hold on to, sometimes to resurrect, recuperate, exhume, the past. Culture is bound to be, to a degree, archaeological. (Think of what we publish today—the most excruciatingly intimate letters of Joyce to his wife, the stories that Kafka insisted should be burned, and so on.) In some ways, then, the editor-critic is, if not our representative, at least our agent, as he develops his plan of campaign to penetrate the old house, bypass or buy off the old lady, and rescue the hidden buried poetry and introduce it into the present, adding it to our culture, our heritage. But he is also a "publishing scoundrel," as Juliana remarks on one memorable occasion when she finds him actually meditating whether to force open a desk which he senses might contain the papers. And there is a central moral problem. The narrator is positively comical as he tries to seduce the old lady and her demure niece (Tita) with endless flowers which he forces the garden to yield (he actually dislikes gardening); and when it comes to, as it were, purchasing the papers indirectly—that too is fair enough. Juliana for him represents "esoteric knowledge" (it is an important part of her mystification that she wears a green eye shade so that—except for one terrible accusing glare when she catches him at the desk—he never sees her properly), and that excites his editorial heart. In just such ways the past is ever seducing the present. And if our editor feels that "my eccentric private errand became a part of the general romance and the general glory" we may mark a note of megalomania, but pass it as understandable all the same. Flowers are harmless. Money is different—that is the source of bargains and there is a great deal of bargaining in the book. Indeed, the old Juliana proves to be a ruthless bargainer, whether over the rent or over a small oval portrait of Aspern which she agrees to sell. Indeed her avidity is her most distinctive characteristic, though the narrator admits that he was possibly responsible for having "lit the unholy flame" of her "coarse cupidity." He is himself, after all, a lesson in avidity when it comes to the Aspern papers. So bargains are fought over and more or less struck. Flowers. Money. But people. . . .

The story changes in tone when the pathetic presence of the unworldly, helpless, friendless niece, Tita, begins to get involved. In a way—we have to decide how calculatingly, how coolly, how cruelly—the narrator does "make love" to Tita, to gain her help in getting access to the papers. He says little enough beyond certain gallantries, but then he is dealing with a lady who has no experience of the world and must be exceptionally impressionable and needy: "From the moment you were kind to her she depended on you absolutely." He is, for mixed motives, kind and she duly becomes absolutely dependent. When Juliana finally dies there is an excruciatingly awkward moment when Tita intimates that her aunt had indicated that Tita could give the narrator the papers if he married her—in effect she offers her hand to him with the promise of the papers in exchange. It is the last of many hard bargains and this time it is a perversion, a degradation. The narrator recoils in barely concealed horror and takes himself off. He now regards Tita as a "piece of middle-aged female helplessness" which he would certainly not encumber himself with. He even loses temper with the confounded Aspern papers—those "crumpled scraps." Then he returns to visit Tita. She is oddly, momentarily "beautified," "angelic," and seems to have acquired a "force of soul," so much so that the narrator thinks to himself, "Why not, after all—why not?" Then Tita reveals that she has burned all the papers—and the transfiguration is over: "she had changed back to a plain, dingy, elderly person." The narrator is left with the oval portrait and his "chagrin at the loss of the letters." How much do we discern him as a scoundrel, how much do we see him as a person in whom values have become so perverted that the papers determine his assessment of another person's worth, or beauty—or simple humanity? How much do we see the "force of soul" in Tita's act of obliterating an inheritance that, as it were, threatened to be more important than her own identity? What do we make of the editor's "eccentric private errand"? These and many other matters James leaves up to the reader—and each reading of this remarkable tale brings out different nuances, different distributions of sympathy. One thing, however, we do recognize, as the narrator himself has to recognize: "I had unwittingly, but none the less deplorably, trifled."

## VII

Much as he admired London and England, James could see that in many ways expressive forms had rigidified into repressive formalities; that it was a society which in its pathological devotion to external proprieties moved inexorably toward the suffocation of personal spontaneity. In such a world conscience could be at a premium and in many of the stories of this period James shows just how hard it was to maintain a true conscience in contemporary society.

One aspect of the Victorian age is that it seemed to enforce an unusually wide gap between the passion cherished in private and the gestures demanded in public (hence so many references to the "buried life" in much poetry and fiction of the time). Concerning this phenomenon, James gave a defining parable in his wonderfully deft "The Private Life" (1892). Ostensibly a mystery story—

Why is a certain great writer (based on Browning) so banal in public, why does a certain famous public figure (based on Lord Leighton) actually seem to vanish when left without an audience?—it has a ghostly resolution that pinpoints the latent schizophrenia of the age. The writer is in fact two people; one a genius who stays in his room and writes in the dark, the other a bourgeois who is his sufficient deputy for dining and gossiping in the "vulgar and stupid" common world. The public figure is indeed so utterly devoted to public appearance ("he had a costume for every function and a moral for every costume") that he has no private life to fall back on. The disguises have absorbed the man. In such an age how should the artist proceed, indeed survive? James returns often to the theme of necessary renunciation. It is the (rather ambiguously given) lesson in "The Lesson of the Master" (1888); it is in "Collaboration" (1892), and a number of other stories—a renunciation not only of public rewards but of domestic consolations. Clearly, James's sense of the possibly enfeebling effects of involvement with women was not diminishing with the years, but his aesthetic is obviously earnestly conceived. Art must "affirm an indispensable truth" and the artist must, like the two collaborators in the story of that name, sacrifice to make that affirmation. Such art "makes for civilization" and ultimately "works for human happiness." James was too aware of so much around him that did not. In fact, the actual visible reality of the age could be insufficient to stimulate true art, as is amusingly brought out in "The Real Thing" (1892), which is something of an ontological joke but with serious resonances. A typical genteel couple in need of money seek work from a book illustrator as models. But they are "all convention and patent-leather." The real thing is the dead thing: it offers no suggestion to the imagination, no scope for "the alchemy of art." The truly "real" is not so easily located and has to be approached by subtler means. The artist cannot confront or, indeed, embrace, his age so directly.

If the Jamesian artist can or must renounce, many of his characters can only succumb. There is little murder in James (though one, in the strange "The Other House"), but there is a surprising amount of death. "Brooksmith" (1891), the butler who develops an artistic imagination, which he cannot employ after his sympathetic master dies, simply withers away. Agatha Grice, torn apart by the forces exerted on her by her English husband and her

American brother commits suicide in "The Modern Warning" (1888). Grace Mavis, the poor American woman who is trifled with and gossiped about on the ship that is taking her to an arranged and unsought-for marriage, jumps overboard in "The Patagonia" (1888). Louisa Chantry, overwhelmed by the shame of revealing a hidden passion, dies almost immediately in "The Visits" (1892). And in one of James's finer stories, "The Pupil" (1891), young Morgan Moreen's heart gives out from an accumulated burden of shame and the sudden shattering impact of a prospective release from his wretched family. Thus society takes its victims.

Something of James's mood during this period may be inferred from his curious story "The Altar of the Dead" (1895). George Stransom is a fairly elderly man, who, since losing his wife, has not only devoted his thoughts to her but also to his other dead friends, as though the dead have become more real and more precious to him than the living. His strongest emotion is a sense of being bereft: he has only one religion—"the religion of the Dead." The dead are close to him, they are "his Dead," and since he "had entered that dark defile of our earthly descent in which some one dies every day," the company of the remembered absent increases continually. One day, after an annual visit to his deceased wife's grave, he enters a church to rest. There he has something like a vision—"he floated away on the sea of light," and the idea of erecting some kind of glowing shrine to his dead takes hold of him, giving him a sense of "a mystery of radiance in which endless meanings could glow." He does indeed gain possession of a vacant chapel in the church and erects an altar on which he places candles to all his dead, keeping the flames burning continually. This is not to be confused with some kind of perverse death worship. It is intended as an act of remembrance, of veneration—a preservation of a sense of the many rare fine human qualities that death is constantly reclaiming. The actual narrative action in this story hinges on the coincidence that a lone woman often keeps her vigil of perpetual mourning at Stransom's altar.

Very gradually they become friends. Then he discovers that the one dead person she is mourning for is a man who was once his greatest friend and then did him an unforgivable wrong (Acton Hague). Since he refuses to put up a candle for Hague, the woman ceases to see him or come to his chapel. He argues with himself that, after all, it is just one more candle—Why not? For by now the lady has become something more than a cherished companion to him. With her absence he feels that "his chapel, in his dreams, was a great dark cavern. All the lights had gone out—all his Dead had died again." He had wanted her to carry on his sacred task when he himself was dead. He falls sick, and on his return to partial health makes a desperate journey to his chapel. It seems that he is never to leave it: "His weakness, his life's weariness overtook him. It seemed to him he had come for the great surrender . . . the very desire to move gradually left him." At this point the lady appears, apparently converted to his idea that the altar should not be for just one, but for all the dead. He in turn speaks of adding one more candle—a concession to her. But we sense that the next and last candle to be added will be for him, for at the end, he lies on the floor of the chapel, and "his face had the whiteness of death." It is a somber, moving, twilight piece, conveying with subtle but almost ceremonial power a mood that prevails in a lot of James's work of his difficult period. It is worth recalling that two of the titles of collections of stories he published during this period were *Embarrassments* (1896) and *Terminations* (1895).

## VIII

In the summer of 1896 James was in a rented cottage in Rye finishing one work and beginning another. The first was to be called *The Other House* (it had an odd history, having started as a play-scenario under the title of *The Promise*, then being turned into a novella, and ten years later converted back again into a play). It is an unusual—and powerful—work in the James canon. For in it he presents us with an almost unmitigatedly evil female figure—the "Bad Heroine," Rose Armiger, who goes far beyond the other women whose complex motivations result in destruction (Christina Light, Madame Merle, Kate Croy). She not only plots and cheats and lies and deceives; she murders a child and then tries to fix the blame on the Good Heroine. The action is precipitated by a vow given by a man, Tony Bream, to his wife on her deathbed—namely that he would not marry again while their child was still alive. Rose Armiger and the "good" Jean Martle are both in love with him, so Rose decides that—since she is willing to do anything to gain possession of Tony—the only way to win him is to kill the child and make it seem that Jean is responsible. It is not melodrama; the passions are vibrant and intense. In giving his account of what happened, Tony looks "as if he were retracing the saddest story on earth." (I wonder if Ford Madox Ford had the phrase in mind for his memorable opening sentence of *The Good Soldier*.) This short and neglected novel has real power, and Rose has a dark force all her own. Almost her last words are defiant: she had seen her chance. Her companion asks, "Chance for what?" She replies: "To make him hate her. You'll say my calculation was grotesque—my stupidity as ignoble as my crime. All I can answer is that I might none the less have succeeded. People *have*—in worse conditions. But I don't defend myself— I'm face to face with my mistake. I'm face to face with it for- ever—and that's how I wish you to see me. Look at me well!" And we do. Of course there is a detectable note here of an actress, a great performance, and it is worth remembering that James was ending a period in which he had immersed himself in the theater. In particular he was at the time under the influence of Ibsen (his friend Elizabeth Robins had played Hedda Gabler in 1891), and James's comments on Hedda Gabler are, as Leon Edel once noted, perfectly applicable to Rose Armiger. James wrote of Hedda: "Her motives are just her passions. . . . She is infinitely perverse . . . one isn't so sure that she is wicked, and by no means sure that she is disagreeable. She is various and sinuous . . . com- plicated and natural; she suffers, she struggles, she is human, and by that fact exposed to a dozen interpretations." *The Other House* is James's most Ibsen-like work and one of the most posi- tive yields of his period as a dramatist.

The other work he was starting that summer and which would be published in 1897 was *The Spoils of Poynton*. Where the former work concentrated on the struggle for possession of a man, this work was to focus on the extraordinary human emo- tions that can be roused by the struggle for the possession of property, valuables, things—"spoils." James's novel—first en- titled *House Beautiful*, then *The Old Things*—certainly addresses itself to what he called "that most modern of our current passions, the fierce appetite for the upholsterer's and joiner's and brazier's work, the chairs and tables, the cabinets and presses, the material odds and ends, of the more labouring ages." The abiding para- dox—the value of beautiful things, the enormities perpetuated on their behalf—is at the very center of this remarkable novel. As James wrote in his later Preface: "The real centre, as I say, the citadel of interest, with the fight waged round it, would have been the felt beauty and value of the prize of the battle, the Things, always the splendid Things." But rather than describe the things directly, he concentrates, wisely, on the passions they arouse. "Yes, it is a story of cabinets and chairs and tables; they formed the bone of contention, but what would merely 'become' of them, magnificently passive, seemed to represent a comparatively vulgar issue. The passions, the faculties, the force their beauty would, like that of Helen of Troy, set in motion, was what, as a painter, one had really wanted of them." The references, even in these few remarks, to citadel, fight, battle, forces, Helen of Troy, added to the many images of combat and spoliation in the book, suggest that James had thought of the Trojan War as a remote but sufficiently apt analogue to his own tale of siege and spoils, invasion and waste. The final conflagration (the house, Poynton, is mysteriously burned to the ground) may deliberately echo the sacking of the city. To the victor the spoils, as we say, but in this battle there are no winners in any traditional sense. Whether any other kind of "victory" can be secured amidst "the ugliness of the whole close conflict" is a question explored by the novel.

The situation that generates the struggle is this: Mrs. Gereth is a widow and it was she who built up the magnificent Jacobean house, Poynton, into a veritable museum of art treasures and fine things. Her husband having died, the house is now in the possession of her son, Owen. He is a powerful but philistine man who doesn't care about "the damned things" (his room full of rifles, whips, tobacco pots—a different kind of collection—is the one "monstrosity" of Poynton). Thus his mother—who cares passionately about the things—is very concerned that he should marry the right kind of woman who would, as it were, maintain the spirit and tradition of Poynton. To this end, she tries to force a young woman, Fleda Vetch, to—in effect—seduce Owen into marriage by giving herself to him. Fleda is too scrupulous, but the crude, sensuous, rapacious Mona Brigstock is not—and she "gets" Owen. And Poynton. This is too much for Mrs. Gereth, who tries various ways of keeping possession of the things—even effectively stealing them at one point. The passions of the three women precipitate the action—they move the unmoving objects, human and material. In terms of a morality play, Mona Brigstock influences Owen through sexual means; Mrs. Gereth uses her worldly cleverness to plot against him; while Fleda Vetch voices the claims of spirituality. He himself—a natural man—seems sufficiently amenable to be Mona's romping partner, Mrs. Gereth's dutiful son, and Fleda's obedient saint. Like the cherished objects that are legally his, he tends to stay where he is put and go where he is pushed. The owner (Owen) is, variously, owned. Products of nature and products of art, here in the form of Owen and Poynton, are in themselves neutral and mindless; everything depends on the resolute temperaments that seek to appropriate them (as Mona does), direct them (as Mrs. Gereth does), or influence them (which is Fleda's "heroic" ambition). In an extreme form we might say that we see physical, mental, and spiritual force variously seeking to influence the inert products of nature and art. The final result is thus of some metaphysical, as well as social, moment.

Mrs. Gereth genuinely appreciates the beauty of "the things." But, as it transpires, she is another of those Jamesian collectors whose humanity has diminished in the dedicated pursuit of things. Fleda can perceive her "almost maniacal disposition to thrust in everywhere the question of Things, to read all behaviour in the light of some fancied relation to them." She is capable of fanaticism and ferocity in her defense of the things; she holds herself like a heroine or a queen among them; she views her guardianship as a sacred duty, thus revealing the extent to which she has confused spiritual and material realms. Her comparatively ruthless obliviousness to the claims of anything (and anyone) outside her things reveals a terrible enslavement to nonhuman matter. Away from the things she seems scarcely to exist—"it took all the light of her treasures to make her concrete and distinct." When she realizes that she has irrevocably lost her things through the marriage of Owen and Mona, she becomes "a dead gray mask," exhausted, "with empty hands in her lap." If things are "the sum of the world," then to lose them is to lose all reason to exist. Mrs. Gereth has been the guardian of her spoils for so long that, as Fleda perceives, it has "despoiled her of her humanity." Fleda disappoints Mrs. Gereth because she will not use her sexuality to catch Owen. It is possible—there are various somewhat neurotic aspects of her behavior—to see Fleda as being in some way pathologically frightened of sex. But this would be far too simple. Better to view it this way: in a world dominated by gestures of acquisition and emotions of possession, Fleda can only express her sense of the existence of superior values through gestures of renunciation and emotions of sacrifice. She is one of those homeless, penniless figures given to lonely meditation who are so important in James: her "only treasure was her subtle mind." She is out of place in the world in which she gets caught up. For her the supreme activities are internal—perception, comprehension, apprehension, sympathy, speculation, that "sense of shades or relations or proportions" that Mona, who is so well suited (and equipped) for action, so strikingly lacks. Fleda's energies are those of imagination rather than appropriation; she muses while the others plot. When she asks herself at one point "What game are they all playing?" we can hear this as the abiding question the spirit asks of those dedicated exclusively to material "games of grab." For Fleda, things, no matter how beautiful, are not the sum of the world.

This is clearly shown when she joins Mrs. Gereth at the lowly house, Ricks, after their defeat. Mrs. Gereth finds the place detestable, but when Fleda comes into the despised cottage she responds to something not on the "inventory" of the furniture which Mrs. Gereth draws up. Fleda tries to define it. "It's a kind of fourth dimension. It's a presence, a perfume, a touch. It's a soul, a story, a life." Fleda is aware of a dimension beyond the purely material.

James was not religious in any orthodox way, and he certainly cherished the beauties of the physical and artistic world, just as he disliked rigid asceticism; but he could see that those who lived exclusively for material ends courted a death of the heart and soul that might go far toward invalidating the beauty of the things they possessed. At the end of the book when Fleda finds the house and all the things devoured by a fire, she says to the stationmaster, "Poynton's *gone*?" To which he makes the considerate and suggestive reply: "What can you call it, Miss, if it ain't really saved?" James leaves his hints as hints, but we are left with the feeling that pure things, unpermeated by spirit, are indeed unredeemed and unredeemable; and that world without soul will not be saved. If the conflagration at Poynton metaphorically looks back to the sacking of Troy, it also carries an anticipatory hint of the Day of Judgment.

In his own Preface James makes it clear that he intends Fleda's "understanding" to be the real focus of the story: "Fleda almost demonically both sees and feels, while the others but feel without seeing." She is a Jamesian spectator, a free spirit among fools— "and the free spirit, always much tormented, and by no means always triumphant, is heroic, ironic, pathetic, or whatever, and, as exemplified in the record of Fleda Vetch, for instance, 'successful,' only through having remained free." Such spectators, passionate in perception, reflection, imagination, typically renounce any share in the spoils of the world (as Strether is to do in *The Ambassadors*). To this extent they are, as James says, "sterile"; indeed, he stresses that everyone in this story is in some way sterile except "the so thriftily constructed Mona." James says, too, that half of Fleda's passion is "wasted and misled" in the activity of subtle considerations, delicate scruples, and fine perceptions. This is the vocabulary of the world, and we can see its aptness. But, confronted by the charred ruins of Poynton, who can say with certainty what is waste and what is gain? There may be something sick about Fleda's addiction to the unseen activities and ungainly motions of conscience—but imagine a world from which all such conscience had fled.

## IX

Problems of possession and conscience are dominant in James's next novel, *What Maisie Knew* (1897)—one of his major works of this period. The situation simply concerns a little girl, Maisie, whose parents (the Faranges) are divorced. They have their various affairs but—not an uncommon phenomenon—they exploit Maisie in various ways, either for their own ends or to anger or to irritate each other. The kindest person to Maisie is Sir Claude, one of Mrs. Farange's lovers, but he is entirely feeble and spineless— no possible kind of father substitute. The other person who claims to care for her is the stern little Mrs. Wix, a type of governess figure who seeks to gain possession of her and, in the end, succeeds. What James centers on is not just the pathos of the exploited little girl, a helpless victim of the sex games that older people play. There is something much more positive to Maisie as she tries to comprehend the world she has to move in. Her most precious attribute—it is a key one in James's work—is her capacity for wonder. As he wrote in the Preface: "The active, contributive, close-circling wonder . . . in which the child's identity is guarded and preserved, and which makes her case remarkable exactly by the weight of the tax on it, provides distinction for her, provides vitality and variety, through the operation of the tax—which would have done comparatively little for us hadn't it been monstrous." The monstrous tax on her wonder is imposed by the selfish, ambiguous, deceptive, exploitative emotions that swirl around her. Her instincts are precisely not selfish. She has "an instinct for keeping the peace," and to this end often practices "the pacific art of stupidity," cultivating a tactful "blankness" in the interests of general harmony and self-preservation. And there is a pathos in her innocence that, because of her situation, is "an innocence so saturated with knowledge and so directed to diplomacy." Yet she is unspoiled by this knowledge: none of the surrounding dirt rubs off on her. Like Fleda Vetch (yet with none of her hysteria), like Verena Tarrant, perhaps even like Daisy Miller, she effectively represents "the only decency" in the world of the book.

But, as well, the book is about Maisie's knowledge—what she sees and what she makes of what she sees. As a child abandoned by her real parents and exploited by her adulterous stepparents, Maisie has more incentive and more need to use her eyes than any other Jamesian character. They are, as it were, all she has. While Maisie would know a great deal if she were an adult, if we remember her limited outlook, her stature, her somewhat vague indiscriminate attention, then we realize how hard it would be for her to read the signs correctly—if at all. As with what she sees, so with what she hears. Out of the confused social murmur sudden phrases detach themselves and come to her ears with a clarity that is as baffling as the previous inaudibility for want of a context: "she found in her mind a collection of images and echoes to which meanings were attachable—images and echoes kept for her in the childish dusk, the dim closet, the high drawers, like games she wasn't big enough to play." Precisely: she lacks the terms, the concepts, the rules of the game, a knowledge of the stakes. She is the recipient of innumerable impressions: but she lacks any coordinating key. True, the novel implies that her mental grasp of the world is constantly growing stronger—"the little girl's interpretations thickened." At the start of chapter 12 we read: "It may indeed be said that these days brought on a high quickening of Maisie's direct perceptions, of her sense of freedom to make out things for herself." Yet, too often enlightenment leads to more enigma. If at one stage she is claiming insouciantly, bravely— " 'Oh yes, I know everything!' "—one of her last pathetic cries is—" 'I don't know—I don't know.' " She develops a sense rather than a sureness "of the relations of things," and it is her reflections that thicken rather than her knowledge of verifiable facts. For James, this could be a very valuable mode of knowledge, an infinitely rich mode of cognition. But of course there is one thing that determines Maisie's groping ignorance, one missing clue without which the whole tangled web of adult involvements will remain forever incomprehensible—sex. She has picked up all the terms, but does not understand the matching substance (this of course generates a lot of the genuine comedy of the book). There is "impropriety"; people can be "compromised"; some people are called "bad": these things she knows, but it is a purely verbal knowledge. For Maisie such words remain almost nonreferential. And as long as the ramifications of sexual appetite are still a mystery to her, her world will remain phantasmagoric, full of sudden events and activities and precipitating motives and mixed consequences that she will never fathom. In a sense the book hinges on what Maisie does *not* know.

Mrs. Wix is the embodiment par excellence of the "conscious conscience," and I think we may infer that Maisie's character might indeed "suffer much" by close association with it, by enforced subjugation to it. Mrs. Wix is constantly upbraiding Maisie for having no moral sense, but she has something more valuable—that sense of wonder. When she first visits Boulogne, her first emotion is "the great ecstasy of a larger impression of life." There is no timidity or fearful holding back: this is the world—this is her world: "She recognized, she understood, she adored and took possession; feeling herself attuned to everything and laying her hand, right and left, on what had been simply waiting for her." The descriptions of the scenes as they appear to Maisie's rapt eye evoke the sensuous delight of the work of the French Impressionists. It is a world that, to Maisie's eye, prances with sheer joy of being. What Maisie has instead of Mrs. Wix's restricting, constricting, negating, prohibiting moral sense is an eagerness of acceptance, a generosity of assimilation, an incorruptible unselfish curiosity, a desire to celebrate life rather than categorize it, a preference for seeing it prancing rather than having it harshly pinned down by rigorous moral judgment. In this novel James is not just saying something about the plight and epistemological problems of an abandoned child: he is also demonstrating what, to him, was the most valuable way of responding to experience—with generous, unselfish wonder. The last word on Maisie, from her creator (in his Preface): "The case being with Maisie to the end that she treats her friends to the rich little spectacle of objects embalmed in her wonder. She wonders, in other words, to the death—the death of her childhood; after which (with the inevitable shift, sooner or later, of her point of view) her situation will change and become another affair, subject to other measurements and with a new centre altogether."

An important novella, again concerned with an isolated young woman, followed in 1898—*In the Cage*. This concerns a young woman who works as a telegraphist in one of the busiest parts of London. By virtue of her situation this heroine is physically almost completely immobilized. She moves around and sees far less than Maisie, and any trip to France would seem to be out of the question. All of her significant activity—except (perhaps) for one notable walk—takes place in her imagination, and here she is much more active even than Maisie. In addition, she is completely excluded from any participation in that area of society that habitually interested James. As he wrote, he had become interested in "the question of what it might 'mean' . . . for confined and cramped and yet considerably tutored young officials of either sex to be made so free, intellectually, of a range of experience otherwise quite closed to them." She is never named, making her more of a presence, a principle, an activity, than a personality and identity. Her actual physical world is real and solid, but elsewhere and irrelevant by virtue of its impoverished low position on the social scale. It consists of a Mr. Mudge and Chalk Farm: that is, physically, where she is condemned to "live." But her imagination lives in Mayfair and it is that which interests James. In this story he has isolated something for special scrutiny. He has devised a situation and manipulated the mechanics of the plot in a way that will exclude all movements and gestures, all situational complexities that might distract from a single focusing; a focusing this time not, as with Maisie, on the wondering eye, but on the wondering imagination. If it was Maisie's vocation to "see," then it is the vocation of this heroine to have visions. Put it another way. Maisie was, to a certain extent, on the outside looking in, through a pane of glass. The telegraphist is on the inside looking out: she is "in the cage," the cage of her isolated imagination. Maisie was to some extent debarred from entering the sweet shop of society: this woman is trapped inside her own head. Her function, we learn, was mainly to "count words as numberless as the sands of the sea, the words of telegrams thrust, from morning to night, through a gap left in the high lattice, across the encumbered shelf that her forearm ached with rubbing."

Telegrams: cryptic hints and compressed signs from the outside world, highly charged fragments from the bustle of society, random dislocated shreds of significance saturated with limitless possible meanings: the heroine's vocation is to *receive*, and in her imagination to *decipher*, telegrams. Her task is that of a Jamesian protagonist in an extreme form.

## X

In September 1897 James signed a twenty-one year lease of Lamb House in Rye. The decision to move from London and to take on, for the first time, a house—an old house—of his own, obviously disturbed James as well as excited him. Certainly in the following four months (September to December 1897) he wrote one of his strangest, most perplexing, haunting stories—"The Turn of the Screw." With a story called "Covering End"—a story version of a play he had written for Ellen Terry—James published the pair in a book with the suggestive title—*The Two Magics*.

Both stories center on old houses, both concern themselves with struggles of possession and dispossession, and in each one a different magic is operative. Covering End is a magnificent old English country house whose legal owner, Clement Yule, has had to mortgage it, so that it is completely in the "possession" of the unscrupulous Mr. Prodmore. Yule meanwhile has taken up radical politics and shown no interest in Covering End—indeed has never seen it prior to the action (one day) of the story. Briefly— Mr. Prodmore wants Clement Yule to give up his radical politics, stand as a Conservative in a safe seat, and marry his daughter Cora. In return he will cancel all the debts on Covering End and restore the house to Yule. On the day of the story he has come to close the deal and Yule is coming to see him at Covering End. But the action is complicated—as far as Prodmore is concerned—by the unanticipated and uninvited presence of a remarkable American woman, Mrs. Gracedew. She, it turns out, is an absolute Anglophile and has made a study of old English country houses and knows more about Covering End than the owner, the old servant, and indeed anybody actually connected with the place. She has come and penetrated the house on her own initiative and is upstairs exploring the old rooms when the other participants foregather.

As it happens, she learns of the "deal" that Mr. Prodmore has proposed and since she regards it as unthinkable that Yule should give up Covering End for radical politics (as he is thinking of doing) she effectively persuades him to accept the bargain that he, admittedly, feels to be "too queer—too cold—too cruel." Fortunately, the apparently docile Cora has broken from her father's influence and has a lover of her own, so she refuses to be party to the squalid deal. That leaves Prodmore, enraged, still in effective possession of Covering End. The key struggle takes place between him and Mrs. Gracedew; she finally buys it from him and gives it to Yule. But Yule has been captivated by "the magic of her manner"—her magic is referred to more than once—and realizes, as he tells her, " 'You saved me.' " Indeed, at an earlier point she had announced to him " 'I'm here for an act of salvation—I'm here to avert a sacrifice,' " and so she does. She wins the struggle for possession of the house and also wins Clement Yule. Her name sufficiently indicates the kind of magic James associates with her—she is a force for regeneration and renewal, effectively reanimating both the house and its owner, bringing new life—and salvation and grace—to both. James was to revert to this theme in *The Golden Bowl*, though in an infinitely more ambiguous manner. One statement of Yule's concerning Covering End will lead us into the companion tale. As Clement Yule walks round the old house of his ancestors for the first time, he says: " 'I don't know what's the matter—but there *is* more here than meets the eye. . . . I miss the old presences. I feel the old absences. I hear the old voices. I see the old ghosts.' " "The Turn of the Screw" hinges, precisely, on someone who, in another ancient house, "sees the old ghosts."

James referred to this story as "a trap for the unwary" as well as a "down-on-all-fours pot-boiler." As to the latter, it is not uncommon for a genius, writing quickly for money, to produce a major work. As to the former, the story has certainly trapped generations of unwary critics and produced more, and more varied, readings and interpretations than any other work by James. Briefly, the story is that a young governess, as her first job, is taken on by a handsome man in Harley Street who wants her to go down to his country house, Bly, and look after his nephew and niece—the only condition being that she must never ever trouble him about them. She goes to Bly, and finds the children, Miles and Flora, enchantingly beautiful, angelic, adorable. One odd note is struck when she learns that Miles has been expelled from his school with no reason given. But to her eyes he is all "love" and the pair of them are figures of absolute innocence. Then the governess sees ghosts, first a man and then a woman. She describes these apparitions to Mrs. Grose, the old housekeeper who has been there for years, and she immediately recognizes them as being the figures of Quint, one of the master's ex-servants, and Miss Jessel, the former governess. Both of these characters are by this time dead. It transpires that Quint and Miss Jessel indulged in a very dissolute life together, and it is quite possible that they corrupted the children, since they had complete control over them. In any case, the governess is convinced that, as evil spirits, they are coming back to take possession of the children, to infect them, and draw them into complete damnation. So she sees her struggle as an attempt to "fence about and absolutely save" the children. To this end she is not only possessive and protective; she tries in different ways—all indirect—to bring the children to the point of confession concerning their contact and dark collusion with Quint and Miss Jessel.

This is where the trouble starts, because it becomes a possibility that the governess—who admits to her "infernal imagination," her "obsession," her susceptibility to impressions, her capacity to be "easily carried away"—is imposing some kind of perverse sexual fantasy on the children. Certainly Flora rebels against her on a crucial occasion when the governess sees Miss Jessel and the child turns accusingly on the governess, saying, " 'I don't know what you mean. I see nobody. I see nothing. I never *have*. I think you're cruel. I don't like you.' " Shortly after this Flora is taken dangerously ill with fever and Mrs. Grose takes her away to London. Alone with Miles, the governess now struggles to save *his* soul, trying to get him to confess to what he had done at school, what really is going on under his innocent appearance. In the climatic final scene, Quint appears at the window and the governess clutches Miles, trying to prevent him from looking in that direction. He is aware of some kind of fearful presence, and there follows an entirely ambiguous exchange. He asks, " 'It's *he*?' " and she quickly asks, " 'Whom do you mean by 'he'?' " Miles replies " 'Peter Quint—you devil!' " The problem here is, to whom is that "you devil" addressed—Quint or the governess? The governess feels triumphant and says " 'What does he matter now, my own? . . . *I* have you, but he has lost you forever!' " But even as she holds him he is dying, and so to the final, memorable sentence. "We were alone with the quiet day, and his little heart, dispossessed, had stopped." Was he saved or suffocated? Did he finally succumb to a powerful evil force reaching from beyond the grave—or was he unable to withstand the tyrannical power of the relentless insinuations of the obsessed governess? Has she been guilty—in her own words—of "the obtrusion of the idea of grossness and guilt on a small helpless creature"? And, as she realizes, "if *he* were innocent, what then on earth was *I*?" Who "possesses" Miles at the end? Quint? the governess? We cannot say. All that is sure is that the little boy's heart is itself "dispossessed" and the ambiguities and ironies that emanate from that perfectly placed word preclude any possible single definitive reading of this tale and the final struggle.

Critics have been quick to pounce on the governess, noting that she has obviously fallen in love with the Harley Street uncle and dreams of doing something heroic to please him; that she is self-confessedly anxious, excessively imaginative and obsessive, and that she is both sexually repressed and overly possessive when it comes to the children (near the end, Miles asks her, very gently, "To let me alone"). If the children are not "angels," they are "fiends" (she was brought up in a vicarage and so all is dramatized into salvation and damnation). Such a figure, the argument goes, would be very liable to hysterical hallucinations and in fact it is she who effectively haunts the children—even to death. There is much in the story to sustain this reading, but it leaves problems. The governess does describe Quint and Miss Jessel without ever having met them. Miles *was* expelled for something at least fairly serious (being an English public school, it could easily, of course, have been for homosexuality). And when Flora is in her fever of hatred concerning the governess, Mrs. Grose admits that her language is " 'really shocking' "—so she has picked up a foul vocabulary somewhere. We must add to this considerations of the form of the story. It is narrated by a friend of the first narrator, and this obviously honorable man has only good things to say about the governess, whom he knew in later life—when she was still a respected and cherished governess. What he then offers is a manuscript of her own account of what happened, and in that account she speaks of "the duty of resistance to extravagant fancies." So there is much support for her honesty and reliability. But of course the question cannot and need not be settled. The whole atmosphere of the house—brilliantly evoked in all its varying moods—does somehow contain a sense of evil, of a bad past, of unsavory secrets, so perhaps the governess can fairly say, with Clement Yule—" 'I feel the old absences. I hear the old voices. I see the old ghosts.' " And somehow, through various agents perhaps, a bad magic is at work, has been at work. Whether the governess "saves" the children, as Mrs. Gracedew "saves" Covering End, is debatable, even dubious: though whether she is responsible for in some way corrupting them with her sick imagination is also debatable and, I would say, dubious. What is certain is that, at the end, Flora is very sick and Miles is dead. This struggle for the possession of human souls has ended only in a fatal "dispossession." And so the story will continue to haunt its readers endlessly—while who knows what personal ghosts James may have been exorcising when he wrote it?

IN JUNE 1898 Henry James moved into Lamb House in Rye. It was there that he was to remain for the rest of his life (apart from some travel), and it was there that he continued his explorations into the problematical depths and intermixings of those "two magics"—the benevolent power for regeneration, the malignant power of destruction—that so wonderfully, so worryingly, make up so much human motivation. The third magic is the art with which he conducted those explorations as he moved into his final phase.

# III

## Lamb House, 1899–1916:

## "The Divine Unrest"

'VE BEEN in London for 3 weeks—came back here on the 20th; and feel the old reviving ache of desire to get back to work. Yes, I yearn for that—the divine unrest again touches me." Thus James in his notebook on January 22, 1899. "Here" was, of course, Lamb House, and there, for the next fifteen years or so the "divine unrest" resulted in some of his greatest works. Not that he stayed uninterruptedly down at Rye. Although he took an active interest in local matters and involved himself a good deal in the provincial life there, he found that he experienced a new kind of loneliness and sense of deprivation—in a word, he missed London, particularly in the winter. So he moved between Rye and London (where he had a series of rooms or apartments) for a decade, finding the former place ideal for work, and the latter, as always, indispensable for stimulation, distraction, and "impressions." It was, it seems, a satisfactory arrangement and between 1902 and 1904 he produced his last three masterpieces—an extraordinary burst of creative energy or "divine unrest." His one major interruption to that life was a visit he made to America in 1904—after an interval of some twenty years. It was not, this time, a visit related to family obligations but rather to "the idea of *seeing* American life again and tasting the American air." To his friend Howells he wrote: "I feel my going not only as a lively desire but as a supreme neces-

sity." He was there for ten months, not only revisiting familiar places but also venturing into the South and out as far as California. In many ways it was a triumphant return, but much of America—like Washington, D.C.—he found to be "a spacious vacancy" and he later recorded his negative feelings and apprehensions about the present and future of his native country in perhaps his most remarkable travel book, *The American Scene* (1907). He was to spend one more year in America after the death of his brother William in 1910, and then he was back to Lamb House—with the attendant fears of the sense of "immobilisation, incarceration" that he intermittently felt there. But there was still London: "Dear old London and its ways and works, its walks and conversations, define themselves as a Prodigious Cure," he wrote.

But the final years were painful. "The evening of life is difficult," he wrote and although at times he could turn, in imagination, back to "the warm and coloured past and away from the big black avenue that gapes in front of us," his life during this period is a series of steps down that black avenue in the protracted and inexorably deepening twilight of his declining years. Of course on one level the period of 1900 to 1916 is the time of his triumph, with recognition coming, if not in the form of palpable royalties (the minute returns on his collected New York edition made him ill), than of the respect in which he came to be held by many of the most important writers of the time, the deference accorded him by a whole range of the most intelligent men and women of his day, and national honors. During this period he met, with varying degrees of pleasure, such writers as Conrad, H. G. Wells, Ford Madox Hueffer (later Ford), Stephen Crane, Edith Wharton (with whom he had one of his most interesting friendships). Socially his contacts ranged from Prime Minister Asquith to Winston Churchill and Virginia Woolf. Among American writers he encountered figures as apparently distant in time as Mark Twain and Ezra Pound. When we remember that in his youth James knew Emerson and Flaubert, we realize what an amazing period of literary richness and innovation he lived through—and contributed to.

But of course it is also the period of sickness and death. One by one, and with increasing rapidity, the lights were going out in the room "of the dusky p.m. of our common existence." James's own health began to let him down—gout, shingles, bad teeth, what was obviously a nervous breakdown (he insisted it was a stomach condition), and a period of intense depression ("I have really been down into hell"). He had one stroke and then another (on this occasion claiming to have heard a voice exclaim, "So here it is at last, the distinguished thing!"), and then there followed a long period preceding his death, when his richly furnished imagination and memory cut adrift and he no longer knew where he was, or, indeed, who he was. At times, Napoleonic fantasies swarmed upon him, and he even signed dictated letters with the name of that emperor who had for so long occupied a unique place in his mind. (It is almost too perfect—or too pathetic—an irony that one of his earliest memories should have been the sight of a Napoleonic column. It is as if that primal and creatively generative memory returned to haunt him as a fantasy or nightmare on his deathbed.) James had staked out his empire in words, vast continents of them over which he reigned as absolute master. No one knows how many compensations go into the thrust that makes an artist create ("the rarest works pop out of the dusk of the inscrutable, the untracked," he himself noted), but James's deathbed hallucinatory fusing of his own identity with that of Napoleon suggests the existence of a profound imperial urge in him which enabled him to go on writing, in absolute solitude, for so long and with such authority. He died on February 28, 1916.

This period of the deaths of relatives and friends culminated in the Great War—"a nightmare from which there is no waking save by sleep." He felt himself to be living under "the funeral spell of our murdered civilization." (It was the war that made him apply for British citizenship, which he acquired on July 28, 1915.) And what he saw as dying was not only all the young men and the social structures of European civilization; language itself, as he understood it, would possibly never recover. It is worth quoting from a remarkable article published in the *Times* in 1915, and unearthed by Leon Edel. Thus James:

The war has used up words; they have weakened, they have deteriorated like motor car tires; they have like millions of other things, been more overstrained and knocked about and voided of the happy semblance during the last six months than in all the long ages before, and we are now confronted with a depreciation of all our terms, or, otherwise speaking, with a loss of expression through increase of limpness, that may well make us wonder what ghosts will be left to walk.

However one reacts to this dire diagnosis, James was right in one thing—after the Great War, literature, perhaps language, could never be the same again.

During the war James often visited the wounded in hospitals, talking to the men much as Walt Whitman had done during the Civil War. James himself made the comparison and it was in his late years that he came to love Walt Whitman's work which, as a youth, he had priggishly dismissed. This change is probably symptomatic of an important feature of the aging James—his avowed homoeroticism (which is not to say that, as far as is known, he was ever a practicing homosexual). Evidence has emerged in recent years of James's intense and manifestly physical (if not actively sexual) feelings for a Norwegian sculptor, Hendrik Andersen. This relationship fades as James realizes the limitations of Andersen's talent, and he warns him explicitly that he is showing signs of megalomania. However, two other relationships seem to have permitted him to express those feelings that at last, and perhaps only in the comparative "safety" of old age, he allowed to surface. These were with Jocelyn Persse and Hugh Walpole. Passion of a kind he now certainly did feel, and Leon Edel is perhaps correct in suggesting that in allowing himself to love and tell his love, James came to reassess the supreme value he ascribed to the act of renunciaton in much of his previous work. So, in the three major fictions of this period—written amazingly in about four years—there is a detectable sense of regret at the life not fully lived (in *The Ambassadors*), a feeling that life without love is no life at all (in *The Wings of the Dove*), and finally a recognition that, despite the many flaws and duplicities in human relationships, marriage can work and produce children who actually stay alive (in *The Golden Bowl*). There is, of course, more to these novels than this, but love and renunciation certainly come under intense scrutiny—and, arguably, revaluation—during this period. Perhaps even more remarkable is the ruthless analysis of the destructive potentialities of egotism, and the terrible death-in-life that can result from the refusal of passional participation in life. This can be found in many of the novels and stories—for example, in "The Beast in the Jungle," in which a Jamesian figure has to confront "the sounded void of his life." If, as seems likely, this story was in part an act of self-examination, then it is a very remarkable and courageous one.

But a central paradox in James's life—a desire to have experience without involvement—remains to the end. Curiosity is curbed by reticence; decorum is punctured by inquisitiveness. He hated "indelicacy" above all things, but could be sedulous in his attempt to discover details about this or that scandal. As the testimony of more than one friend reveals, he yearned to know the full horrors of life, but could scarcely bear to hear them named. In a letter referring to a visit to the house where George Sand had lived with her lovers, James refers to it as the place "where they pigged so thrillingly together." The uniquely Jamesian collocation of words is, of course, extremely amusing; at the same time, it is characteristic in the absolute duality of response that it reveals. A part of James obviously experienced nausea and dread at the idea of people "honeying and making love / over the nasty sty." Another part of him found the whole mystery surrounding the most intimate of human contacts "thrilling." In another man, the results could have been merely an unhealthy prurience. And perhaps James did suffer from an insufficiency of physical experience. (R. D. Laing's comment that "the unembodied self engages in nothing directly . . . the unembodied self becomes hyper-conscious" might be relevant here.) But there is no legislating for art, no prescribing for the artist, and James's curious combination of empathy and detachment enabled him to achieve miracles of insight into the nuanced and elusive procedures of consciousness as it attempts to cope with the mystifications and conflicts inherent in civilized living.

## II

The first novel that James wrote after his move to Rye was *The Awkward Age*, and interestingly—though not perhaps surprisingly—it stresses the perverse corrupting atmosphere of London society and the blessings of a rural retreat. It is a book that hinges on two kinds of "innocence"—that irresistible, ambiguous state in James—as represented by two different young girls who are, precisely, at "the awkward age"—no longer children, not yet women (the state of sexual limbo is clearly intended). Nanda is like a somewhat older Maisie, though the oppressive social fogs, the adult "malaria" in which she lives and through which she moves is a more suffocating and sordid medium than Maisie's world. She is a girl who has been too carelessly "initiated," who "knows everything" (that ironic recurring phrase in James), and yet whose "precious freshness of feeling" seems uncorrupted by the squalid ethos to which her eyes are so candidly, so clearly open. Yet she is rejected by the fashionable world in the character of Vanderbank (whom she loves). He feels that she has been too long steeped in a poisonous atmosphere to which, it must be stressed, he has largely contributed. It is important to note that Nanda's mental pollution or contamination—if that is what it is—can be traced to her reading of a French book Vanderbank set in circulation in the social group that centers on Mrs. Brookenham (the volatile, adroit, morally ambiguous mother of Nanda and, incidentally, James's own favorite among the characters he created). No title of the book is given but Zola is the one author referred to—by Vanderbank himself—so we may guess at both its tone and content. (The only book title referred to is *Anna Karenina*, which, in a novel obsessed with the possibilities of adulterous sexuality, speaks for itself.) It is a fine touch that has Nanda write Vanderbank's own name on the cover of the untitled book, because in a very real sense he *is* the "author"—the point of origin—of Nanda's mental "rape" or seduction. If she is the "drain pipe" she thinks she is, it is largely because Vanderbank has helped to pour the literary "dirt" into her home atmosphere. The book is later used in a very physically sexual, illicit game—by Aggie after her marriage. But Nanda remains a paradoxical figure—at once violated and virginal. When the socially glib—but humanly blank—Vanderbank refuses to accept this paradox of knowledge-in-innocence, it is a case of an author's rejecting one of his own creations who has grown too complex for him. James, the other "author," can both create and accept her. Indeed, we might note here a curious but critical similarity between James and Nanda. The other source of Nanda's so-called knowledge is the "talk" going on around her. But that talk is so marked by gaps, hesitations, ellipses, incompletions, and evasions that by the end we have the feeling it is largely nonreferential. Delicacy of specification becomes absence of signification. Sex is certainly in the air; but in this social world "We all call everything—anything."

Indeterminacy of nomenclature becomes total semantic deple-tion: "if that's what you call talking—never saying a word," as Mr. Longdon (see below) justifiably remarks. What can Nanda *really* "know" about sex from written fictions and social utter-ances that are at once allusive and vacuous? But then—and this is a question of some importance—what could James himself "know" (given that, as is generally accepted, he had no hetero-sexual experience) apart from what he inferred from books and talk—and silences? Being James he inferred a great deal and with more subtlety than most sexually initiated writers. But the fact remains that in his "knowing" innocence or innocent "knowing-ness" he is oddly like Nanda. It is perhaps not surprising that he seems particularly sympathetic and protective toward her.

The other girl, Aggie, is brought up in a state of total ignorance. She "isn't exposed to anything," she has been kept from coming "downstairs" by her socially scrupulous mother, the duchess. Her eyes are blinkered and averted from any tell-tale evidence of the adult world. She reads history "that leaves the horrors out": she is sedulously preserved from all possibly polluting contacts. She is brought up in a garden of innocence, apart from the contaminated society in which she is subsequently to live; whereas from the start Nanda (who *has* come "downstairs," i.e., into adult society) recognizes that "we're in society, aren't we, and that's our hori-zon" and she faces the fact by not feigning a sly ignorance but accepting things as they are for what they are. Hence her "crude young clearness," a clearness that is not muddied by what it sees and learns.

Two innocents: the real and the apparent, the plainly honest and the prettily plausible, the seemingly knowing and the seem-ingly ignorant: what happens to them? Here we must bring in the character of Mr. Longdon. He is a Jamesian spectator, "a fresh eye, an outside mind," in this case not from America but from an ideal past of taste, kindliness, and decorum. He has—just like Henry James!—a beautiful walled garden in a house in the country. He spends much of his time trying to appraise the respec-tive innocences of Nanda and Aggie through the murk of a society with which he no longer feels in sympathy.

Both girls struck him as lambs with the great shambles of life in their future; but while one, with its neck in a pink ribbon, had no consciousness but of being fed from the hand with the small sweet biscuit of unobjectionable knowledge, the other struggled with instincts and forebodings, with the suspicion of its doom and the far-borne accent, in the flowery fields, of blood.

When Aggie—in her "pink ribbon"—does finally come downstairs and out into society, it is "with a bound—into the arena." Even before her honeymoon is over, she is engaging in adulterous sexual games of tooth and claw with a predatory vigor and immorality that justify James's strong animal imagery. So much for the traditional innocent. Nanda moves in the opposite direction: the more she sees and knows, the more society conspires to exclude and abandon her. There is a real pathos in the manner in which her fate starts to take on a definite shape toward the end of the book until she finally returns "upstairs": her punishment for having "unlearned surprise" and for not practicing a false ingenuousness. However, she is not left to suffocate upstairs. When Vanderbank finally abandons her, Mr. Longdon comes to her rescue and invites her to come away with him to his rural paradise, though he imposes one rather stern condition. "You understand clearly, I take it, that this time it's never again to leave me—or to *be* left." He is indeed offering a retreat: a total retreat from social life, from its battles and nightmares, but also from its possible richness and fulfilments. Nanda however is well schooled in renunciation. Early in the book she seems lucidly aware of her doom and she says of marriage: "I shall be one of the people who don't. I shall be at the end . . . one of those who haven't." She has had her "one crowded hour of glorious life" but—and here we approach a basic Jamesian theme, one that he was to reexamine in subsequent works—just because she has opened her eyes to all of it, just because of her unprejudiced lucidity of vision, she seems to forfeit all rights of participation, all the privileges of consummation. Henry James, in the form of Mr. Longdon, enters his own novel to rescue Nanda, as though, recognizing the value of her attitude toward life and the pathos of her predicament, he could not bear to see her so foolishly undervalued and so callously marooned. But he was to think again about renunciation and retreats.

His next novel was to be the most enigmatic he ever wrote—indeed, Edmund Wilson suggested that if we could really understand *The Sacred Fount* (1901), we would have got to the heart of Henry James's secret—if one wants to think of a great artist having a secret rather than being aware of endless ambiguities. The novel centers on a weekend social gathering at a house in the country—Newmarch; and the first-person narrator is a solitary figure who is in some ways an outsider in the house who ends by fleeing from it, as if from society itself. This figure is unnamed, undescribed, more of a consciousness than a participant. What we make of this book depends on how we regard the activity of this consciousness while it is in the house, endlessly trying to work out the real relationships between the various visitors (again the problem is quite obviously, if implicitly, the matter of sexual and passional relationships). He has been variously regarded as an intolerable busybody, a sterile figure of chilling prurience, a victim of insane delusions and vanities, a veritable death's head in the house of life. On the other hand, he has also been taken to embody the whole artistic instinct, and his activities have been seen as a parable of the way the artist elicits aesthetic order out of human chaos. He has been seen as both the curse and conscience of society—and perhaps no one of these readings need necessarily exclude all the others. James may well have been peering and probing into what his activity really was as an observer/writer. The theory that the narrator tries to apply to the tangled and concealed relationships at Newmarch is one to which James, to some extent, also subscribed. It is based on the idea of one person nourishing himself (or herself) on another's life energy (a kind of vampirism), so that what one gains in vitality another may be losing. (This secret replenishing source is the "sacred fount" of the title, which also alludes to the sacred springs of the Italian goddess Egeria, who nourished King Numa. He is mentioned in the book.) The narrator notes that one lady, Grace Brissenden, seems to have grown suddenly much younger, while her husband seems to be unrecognizably old and tired; noticing also that a usually stupid man named Gilbert Long seems to be manifesting unusual wit and flair, he begins to look for some depleted victim who must be paying for this improvement. His speculations and searchings are sometimes corroborated by other people, sometimes dismissed as being unhealthy and intrusive, sometimes challenged and denied. Having decided that the fourth member of the algebraic pattern is one Mrs. Server, he builds his whole "palace of thought" around this surmise. In this at least he is obsessive, monomaniacal; it is clearly suggested that other pairings, groupings, relations are possible.

In a brilliant touch at the end, the narrator reveals that suddenly he feels immensely old and drained—perhaps on one level, he himself has been drained by his chief antagonist, the triumphant Mrs. Brissenden! As the narrator discovers, other people have other readings, other theories that are "alien" and "insoluble" in his particular construct. "Vast, truly, was the world of observation, that we could both glean in it so actively without crossing each other's steps." The possibility of everyone gleaning a different picture of the state of things from the vast world of observation is increased by the extraordinarily elliptical and unspecific nature of the social language used by them all. The narrator, sensing the discrepancy between the surfaces of the social charade, and the "things unspoken and untouched, unspeakable and untouchable" that lie behind, tries to make himself an expert in the semantics of silence—reader of the unwritten, hearer of the unsaid. There are obvious dangers in such an endeavor. Mrs. Brissenden has a point when she rebuffs him with the scornful comment: "things are not gouged out to your tune." And obviously James could see that there is a real danger in becoming so totally enthralled with one's own theory of things. And yet clearly there is a value in the sort of consciousness that tries to fathom some of "those suppressed processes and unavowed references which made the meaning of the meeting so different from its form." James himself could hardly have disdained such a description of his own aspirations as a novelist. Near the end, the narrator says to Mrs. Brissenden: "Light or darkness, my imagination rides me." The whole motive and momentum of the artistic imagination are just as ambiguous as that. It is not always possible to tell those efforts of the mind that illuminate existence from those that darken it.

Quite early in the book the narrator willingly concedes: "These things—the way other people could feel about each other, the power not one's self, in the given instance, that made for passion—were of course at best the mystery of mysteries; still, there were cases in which fancy, sounding the depths or the shallows, could at least drop the lead." Comic, pathetic, deranged, pathological, sympathetic—however the characters, or we, choose to regard the narrator, we should recognize that whether he is right or wrong (he could, after all, be correct), his attempt to find patterns in the shifting relationships around him, his efforts to sound the depths of that "power not one's self . . . that made for passion," are only another version of what Henry James, like most great novelists, was doing himself. If this is madness then it is, in James's own phrase, "the madness of art."

### III

"Frankly, quite the best, 'all round,' of my productions," was James's own assessment of *The Ambassadors*, written in about ten months in 1900. It centers on a man, very much of James's age and disposition, who is sent to Europe to retrieve a young man, Chad, from what his excessively moralistic mother (Mrs. Newsome) regards as inevitable corruption in Europe. But the man, Lambert Strether, has an epiphany or a "crisis" of vision in Paris and breaks out to another young man with these central words: "Live all you can; it's a mistake not to. It doesn't so much matter what you do in particular so long as you have your life. If you haven't had that, what *have* you had. I'm too old—too old at any rate for what I see. What one loses one loses; make no mistake about that . . . I'm a case of reaction against the mistake. Do what you like so long as you don't make it. For it *was* a mistake. Live, Live!" "Mistake" is a key recurring word, and the questions of the nature of Strether's mistake, and of whether he can yet make any reparation, constitute the central interest—and drama—of the novel. A crucial problem—or endless ambiguity—is, of course, What exactly *is* it to live? So that you *have* your life? On such central questions the book, through Strether, ponders with extraordinary subtlety and delicacy. It is in *The Ambassadors* that James, for the first time, makes the consciousness of the onlooker the central focus of a major novel. Discussing his initial conception of Strether, James wrote: "He would have issued, our rueful worthy, from the very heart of New England" and "he had come to Paris in some state of mind which was literally undergoing, as a result of new and unexpected assaults and infusions, a change from hour to hour." It is a central Jamesian theme: a person confronting new facts with an old vision, or set of values or system of belief, and experiencing a convulsion of values because the old "vision" will not adequately account for the newly perceived facts. Thus, James goes on, "the false position for him . . . was obviously to have presented himself at the gate of that boundless menagerie with a moral scheme of the most approved pattern which was yet framed to break down on any approach to vivid facts." The book, then, is to be about an approved moral scheme challenged by confusing vivid facts, and the consequent attempt to find a new adequate scheme, a more inclusive vision that can contain the new range of facts even if it loses its old approval. The drama is to be "the drama of discrimination." How excessively narrow and life-denying is the New England conscience? What is fine and what is fraudulent in the rich aggregation of life's possibilities that Paris represents? The book is, as James says, about a revolution of consciousness in Strether, a revolution that has nothing to do with any carnal temptations offered by Paris, but is rather about its power to stimulate the sensitive and appreciative imagination, to feed the senses with rich and novel impressions. It is notable that on at least three important occasions Strether is depicted meditating alone on a balcony ("a perched privacy appeared to him the last of luxuries"), taking in, as it were, the whole scene. As he looks down on one occasion, James writes "Strether found himself in possession as he had never yet been": visual possession, possession from above. A possession that is generous and grateful—nonexploitative.

There are a number of American "ambassadors" (note the plural title) and for the most part they refuse Europe, judging and condemning—never trying to appreciate. And yet they are also enthusiastic purchasers and collectors (in its way a power gesture—reducing Europe to a shop and treating it like a contemptuous patron). Strether is a notable nonpurchaser. Behind the ambassadors is Mrs. Newsome, who is also the employer of Strether. She is—the image is used—a moral "iceberg." From her, through other characters, emanates a steady cold force of disapproval and self-righteous negation. She gets all her money from a vulgar business which, it is implied, won its power through corrupt means. The combination of unscrupulous commercial exploitation and moral self-congratulation is clearly established. Over against her is the—ultimately pathetic—figure of Madame de Vionnet, who incorporates the distilled essence of an old European civilization. She is Chad's mistress. Mrs. Newsome and all the other ambassadors try—they threaten financial punishment as well as moral disapproval—to force Strether to return to America. In not returning when they return, Strether is refusing their attitude to life. He stands firm—stands by Madame de Vionnet, stands by the perceptible, as opposed to the purchasable, values of Europe.

The worst ambassador will turn out to be Chad. He is completely egotistical: as he claims, he has always had his own way. He is a "taker" supreme, for he takes and keeps and uses all the love and care that Madame de Vionnet lavishes on him—with no true reciprocations. Because Chad has acquired a European veneer and to some extent been civilized by Madame de Vionnet, Strether is initially taken in by Chad's improved appearance. But by the end he can perceive that Chad is really just another one of those Americans who have come to Europe to exploit its valuable things before returning to America and the profits of big business. Chad's intention to return to America is not announced but clearly inferred. By the end Strether is trying to work on Chad to keep him in Europe (a major ironic reversal, since earlier Chad has to work on Strether to gain his permission to stay longer in Europe), and he feels it necessary to utter a strong prospective indictment: "You'll be a brute, you know—you'll be guilty of the last infamy—if you ever forsake her." Chad glibly says that he will never tire of her, but "he spoke of being 'tired' of her almost as he might have spoken of being tired of roast mutton for dinner." A rank selfishness of mere appetite is hinted at here. And even while Strether is showing him how vile it would be to abandon Madame de Vionnet, Chad suddenly switches the conversation to "advertising": "It really does the thing, you know"—the "thing" being to make money. He is still oblivious to intrinsic values. What for Madame de Vionnet is a real and lasting love is for him a passing amusement to be indulged in before going into business.

But she has a sort of wisdom that the egotistical American ambassadors could never attain. As when she says "What I hate is myself—when I think that one has to take so much to be happy, out of the lives of others, and that one isn't happy even then. . . . The wretched self is always there, always making one somehow a fresh anxiety. What it comes to is that it's not, that it's never, any happiness at all, to *take*. The only safe thing is to give." She has given, and, we feel, she alone of the characters will achieve the dignity and stature of real suffering. But only Strether can really appreciate her for what she is. And he too attempts to transcend "the wretched self" by refusing to take anything that the world seems to offer—including two possible and very secure and comfortable marriages. For in the Jamesian world, those who consult and pander to the self are capable of cruel obliquities of vision and a ruthless insensitivity of conduct. Really "living" is a subtler affair than that. Strether *does* "have his life"—in the form of accumulated treasures of consciousness and capacious generosities of vision.

At one point he visits Madame de Vionnet (after he has discovered that she and Chad are lovers): he perceives her fear and achieves an ethical sense that goes far beyond a mere disapprobation for a socially illicit deed. His fine insight (James calls it "his sharpest perception yet") is that "it was almost appalling, that a creature so fine could be, by mysterious forces, a creature so exploited." It is the "exploitation" of people that is the cardinal sin in the Jamesian world: evil is the callous manipulation and selfish appropriation of other peoples' lives—of life itself. For such people—such as most of the American ambassadors, supremely Chad—it is not a matter of "living all you can," but rather of "getting" all you can. With his acquired subtlety of vision and refined ethical sense—and pity—Strether by the end approaches very close to the Jamesian view of the world—and, indeed, by the end, the values of character and author would seem to overlap to a large extent. This leaves one interesting question. Why does Strether, at the end, go back to America? Madame de Vionnet's question is very relevant here. She asks him: "Where *is* your home moreover now—what has become of it?" The "unhomeing" of Strether is important. His vision is now too wide and comprehensive to be limited to commitment to—identification with—any one home. Just as, from the balcony the watcher is "well out of it," but most aware of it all going on. In addition, in a strange Jamesian way, "it was he somehow who finally paid, and it was the others who mainly partook." He seems to become the containing, all-embracing consciousness of the various participants; but he must pay by forfeiting his place on the stage. That is what is behind the reason he gives for not staying in Europe. In going back to America he is, it is made very clear, going back to completely nothing—a blank, a nowhere. But that is the whole point. He explains: "But all the same I must go. . . . To be right. . . . That, you see, is my only logic. Not, out of the whole affair, to have got anything for myself." He must not appear to have opted for one culture as opposed to the other. It is not to be simply a matter of changing sides—it is getting beyond sides altogether, and the geographical equivalent of this is his refusal to seek around for a comfortable corner for himself in Europe. To show that Strether's vision has passed beyond all the demands of "the wretched self," it is important that he must not get any material loot or swag for himself (as, for instance, even his friend Maria Gostrey has her little museum of sharp acquisitions). He must be above all collecting, all purchasing, all possessing. His gain must be all of the imagination, even if there does seem to be something excessively ascetic in this attitude; what he *has* acquired are gems of appreciation, understanding, and a range of sympathy that transcends any fixed moral schemes. Thus we have our last glimpse of Strether looking, perhaps, not unlike James himself—alone, "unhomed" in a profound sense, somehow out of life, but full of a priceless vision.

## IV

As mentioned earlier, James had a young cousin, Mary Temple, a brilliant, life-hungry girl who died tragically young. She became the very image of a generous but doomed consciousness, which James was to explore and dramatize in different ways. He wrote of her in his *Notes of a Son and Brother*:

> She was absolutely afraid of nothing she might come to by living with enough sincerity and enough wonder. . . . Life claimed her and used and beset her—made her range in her groping, her naturally immature and unlighted way from end to end of the scale. . . . None the less she did in fact cling to consciousness; death, at the last, was dreadful to her; she would have given anything to live—and the image of this, which was long to remain with me, appeared so of the essence of tragedy that I was in the far-off aftertime to seek to lay the ghost by wrapping it . . . in the beauty and dignity of art.

This he most beautifully did in *The Wings of the Dove,* which he wrote immediately after *The Ambassadors* (though it was published one year before that novel, in 1902).

Mary Temple is transformed into Milly Theale, who is a young American princess, "an angel with a thumping bank account," indeed—"a dove." But she is mortally ill when she comes over to Europe, though she is desperately eager to "live." She enters the novel only with Book 3 and thereafter she hardly acts, but is, rather, acted upon. The novel in fact starts with another lady— the English woman, Kate Croy, who indeed initiates much of the action—and she is one of the very great studies of a woman in English fiction. The first sentence unostentatiously points to some of the key aspects of the novel: "She waited, Kate Croy, for her father to come in, but he kept her unconscionably. . . ." "Waiting" is one of the problems of the book—Kate, for instance, is secretly engaged to a penniless journalist, Merton Densher, but as she herself has no money, they cannot get married. And they have no place to go. So they must wait—and the other problem is, exactly what is "conscionable" or "unconscionable." Milly has "boundless freedom" and is indeed first seen high in the Alps, climbing a path that "led somewhere, yet apparently quite into space"—she can indeed spread her wings and fly where she will. She is associated with large rooms, ample houses, and a superb elevated Italian palazzo in Venice—where she eventually dies.

Kate, however, seems condemned to cramped and mean settings—her father's squalid rooms in Chirk Street, her sister's no less squalid house—in neither of which is she wanted. She is accepted at the massively splendid house, Lancaster Gate, home of Aunt Maud. But—and here is Kate's problem—Aunt Maud is a veritable "lioness," an "eagle" with predatory talons all exposed. She is "a complex and subtle Britannia," sitting imperiously among her ostentatiously material possessions: "she *was* London, *was* life—the roar of the siege and the thick of the fray." And she is determined that Kate should marry not the impoverished Densher, but the rich Lord Mark. Kate is a complex woman in an impossible position. She recognizes that "material things spoke to her" and is not out of this world, as the more ethereal Milly is. At the same time, she is loyal to Densher and *does* commit herself to him: "I engage myself to you forever," she announces. But they are without a place—they meet in art galleries, in parks, even on the underground railway: public places of passage hardly constituted to offer lovers privacy. So Kate plots— in the subtlest way. She becomes a friend of Milly's—a "sincere" friend—and realizes that she is going to die. She also realizes that Milly—who has never really been properly loved or known love—is falling in love with Merton Densher. So she subtly suggests to Densher that they continue to conceal their engagement and that he should marry Milly—and thus soon inherit her fortune. "Since she's to die, I'm to marry her?" he asks. "To marry her," Kate replies. "So that when her death has taken place I shall in the natural course have money?" "You'll in the natural course have money," Kate concludes. "We shall in the natural course be free." The plot is not so purely Machiavellian as it may sound. On the one hand, Kate sincerely wants Milly to be happy for the short time she has left, but it goes wrong when Lord Mark, in a spirit of revenge (he has been rejected by Milly), reveals to her the secret engagement of Kate and Densher. Because of this, so we gather, in a famous statement—"She [Milly] has turned her face to the wall." She does, in fact, leave her money to Densher, but something has happened to him and he now cannot touch it and will only marry Kate on that condition.

"I'll marry you, mind you, in an hour."
"As we were?"
"As we were."

But she turned to the door, and her headshake was now the end. "We shall never be again as we were!"

So the novel famously concludes. They have lost their love and their future. Milly has escaped into the great space of death. They are left alone back "in the same box. Their box, their great common anxiety, what was it, in this grim breathing-space, but the practical question of life?" It might be stressed that the problems of place and space, direction and "position," "journey" and "flight," "abyss," "labyrinth," and "maze" are prominent throughout. The various rooms and houses and galleries through which Milly and the others pass do add up both to a kind of "social atlas" and to a whole social, psychological, and moral geography, until the late great scene in the stormy Venice in winter—"It was a Venice all of evil that had broken out for them alike"—when Densher is turned away from Milly's palazzo and realizes that his lie and deception have been exposed. The final sense of desolation and loss is very intense.

The problem of the lie is central to the book. No one knew better than James that society is maintained and structured on varying degrees of fiction, fabrication, suppression, misrepresentation—a whole scale of collusion and duplicity. Yet, particularly in connection with human relationships, the lie can be ruinous. The notion of lying (and "playing the game" of society) is there from the start when Kate meets her father—a man with some disgrace in his past—and realizes "there was no truth in him . . . he dealt out lies as he might have cards from the greasy old pack for the game of diplomacy to which you were to sit down with him." When she assures Milly that she has no feeling for Densher, she reports to Densher, "I've told the proper lie for you." Is there such a thing as a "proper lie"? In Venice, Densher, increasingly frustrated that he is having to enact Kate's plot while she still won't come to bed with him, says: "I'll tell any lie you want . . . if you'll only come to me." And come she does. But there is a point when he can no longer lie and deny his love for Kate. Kate sees it differently. Milly, she says, "never wanted the truth. . . . She wanted *you*. . . . You might have lied to her from pity." It is plausible but specious. Densher has realized that there comes a point when the lying has to stop, recognizing, like various other characters in fiction (Mark Twain's Huck Finn, Conrad's Razumov), that, finally, you can't live a lie. As he says to Kate after Milly's death, "we've played our dreadful game, and we've lost"—he leaves the letter announcing Milly's bequest to him unopened, signifying a renunciation of the money. Kate *has* her sincerities and her truths—she *has* been faithful to her love for Densher. But she cannot escape the box—of materiality, and perhaps, unavoidably, of mendacity, in which she has to live. Milly, freed from the start from all material worries and restrictions, has to die. Densher is left with, perhaps, a new conscience, a memory, and the prospect of an endless solitude.

At one point in Lord Mark's great country house, Matcham, Milly is shown a Bronzino portrait of a woman. The day has been perfect—"a sort of magnificent maximum, the pink dawn of an apotheosis," and indeed the world does seem "all before her" (James uses the Miltonic echo as he had in *The Portrait of a Lady*).

Yet the moment of apotheosis is also a presentiment of doom. In front of the picture she finds she is "looking at the mysterious portrait through tears."

> Perhaps it was her tears that made it just then so strange and fair—as wonderful as he had said; the face of a young woman, all magnificently drawn, down to the hands, and magnificently dressed; a face almost livid in hue, yet handsome in sadness and crowned with a mass of hair rolled back and high, that must, before fading with time, have had a family resemblance to her own. The lady in question, at all events, with her slightly Michelangelesque squareness, her eyes of other days, her full lips, her long neck, her recorded jewels, her brocaded and wasted reds, was a very great personage—only unaccompanied by a joy. And she was dead, dead, dead. Milly recognised her exactly in words that had nothing to do with her. "I shall never be better than this."

Thus was Mary Temple wrapped, in this incomparable novel, "in the beauty and dignity of art."

While meditating his next novel James wrote a book about the American expatriate artist William Wetmore Story. He called the book a "queer job" and it is indeed an unusual mixture of biography, documents, and autobiographical reminiscences. James never had much respect for Story as an artist, but he undertook the book for financial reasons (and under some pressure from Story's children), and wrote it in about two months (his work rate during this last major phase is simply amazing). The full title of the book is *William Wetmore Story and His Friends: From Letters, Diaries, and Recollections*, and as Edel has said, the key word is "recollections." James had first experienced Rome at the time when Story was working there, so he plunges into his own recollections of the impact of Rome on an aspiring American artist in the middle of the nineteenth century. It was a time when Americans, in an almost naïve and childlike way, were beginning to discover Europe for the first time: "The dawn of the American consciousness of the complicated world it was so persistently to annex is the more touching the more primitive we make that consciousness . . . the interest is in its becoming perceptive and responsive, and the charming, the amusing, the pathetic, the romantic drama is exactly that process." It was a drama that James had traced out many times. More important to James than Story was the whole atmosphere of Rome, in particular as it contrasted with the air of moral fear and foreboding in New England. Referring to "the suspended *fear* in the old, the abiding Puritan conscience," James alludes to the old image of "the whip in the sky" and adds "from the Italian sky of those days the whip was, in respect to all of its functions, blissfully absent."

Yet interestingly enough, James reveals, in discussing Story, some of his abiding sense of the ambiguous results of expatriation. It is not exactly clear what or how much he is confessing when he asserts that "a man always pays, in one way or another, for expatriation, for detachment from his plain primary heritage," and after recording some of the felicities of Story's Roman life, he asserts that "Story *paid*—paid for his having sought his development even among the circumstances that at the time of his choice appeared not only the only propitious, but the only possible." Something, somehow, is missing from Story's work—"Story therefore affects us as concurring, curiously, almost perversely, in some fine extravagant waste or leakage." It is strange to read the long-committed expatriate James commenting thus on a fellow expatriate, and one can only wonder to what extent he might be indirectly referring to something he felt about himself. But whatever the long-term results of expatriation may be, there is no mistaking the sheer golden magic of Rome—evoked by James in this book with an intensity of appreciative nostalgia that is truly creative.

> So, at any rate, fanciful as my plea may appear, I recover the old sense—brave even the imputation of making a mere Rome of words, talking of a Rome of my own which was no Rome of reality. That comes up as exactly the point—that no Rome of reality was concerned in our experience, that the whole thing was a rare state of the imagination, dosed and drugged, as I have already indicated, by the effectual Borgia cup, for the taste of which the simplest as well as the subtlest had a palate.

It is the fine intensity of James's own recollections, and his incomparable "Rome of mere words," that transcend his ostensible material—William Story—and make this book a worthy, though underrated, product of his major phase.

## V

In his last great novel, *The Golden Bowl* (1904), James concentrates on two married couples almost to the exclusion of anyone else (there are very few, and only minor, other characters). It is as if society has receded far beneath them, is barely audible in the rarefied atmosphere in which they move. In a sense they are making their own society, and their efforts to do this—with a success that may be seen as ambiguous or redemptive—constitute the quiet but intense drama of the book (the only real noise occurs when Maggie smashes "the golden bowl." But she immediately starts to pick up the pieces). It is a curiously "geometrical" book dealing with shifting combinations, groupings, "ruptures and rearrangements," "reconstitutions" (which, ideally, should be "plausible, presentable"), and a general concern for "equilibrium." The book starts with two licit relationships; these shift into illicit or unnatural relationships; then there is a "rearrangement" and a return to two legitimate relationships. Though, of course, by the end the characters have all changed and are in very different situations of knowledge and power. They can never be again as they were. But, and here we do have something new in James, the two marriages *have* survived as indeed has the one child produced by the unions. James was originally going to call the novel *The Marriages*, and it is a key word and, indeed, key relationship in the book ("I want to *be* married. It's—well, it's the condition," says one of the ladies prior to her actually entering that state). On what terms and in what state the marriages survive is very much a matter for debate, and indeed there has been the widest possible disagreement about this since the novel appeared. Either the characters are preserved—some say redeemed—by the maintaining of the forms; or, it has been argued, the forms are maintained at the expense of the characters. I will come back to this.

Put very simply, the story concerns a young rich American woman, Maggie Verver (some have seen a regenerative hint in the "Ver"—Latin for spring—and I suppose you could find more than a hint of English verve or vigor), who is married to an Italian prince, Amerigo. A former friend (lover?) of the prince turns up, Charlotte Stant, initially to buy them a wedding present. The prince and Charlotte, it need hardly be said, are poor, so even if they had wanted to get married in the past it was financially out of the question—not a new situation in James! Maggie's father, Adam, joins them and—really for the sake of symmetry, or as he thinks, for the sake of his daughter's marriage—he marries Charlotte (he is, incidentally, revealed as sexually impotent, so they can have no child). But it doesn't work out quite as it should. Maggie and Adam become closer and closer, a slightly unnatural father-daughter intimacy that is only intensified when Maggie has a child (he is a "link between a mamma and a grandpapa"—but not between a wife and her husband). The prince and Charlotte are left to themselves—indeed, rather thrust at each other—and almost inevitably they commit adultery and become lovers. In a way they set up a new kind of contract, since the other marriages seem to have gone off in somewhat perverse, or at least unful-filling, directions. "We must act in concert, Heaven knows . . . *they* do!" says Charlotte, and their passion, as demonstrated in their kiss, seems to give the "contract" a kind of validity. "Their lips sought their lips, their pressure their response and their response their pressure; with a violence that had sighed itself to the longest and deepest of stillnesses they passionately sealed their pledge." Maggie and Adam are said, indeed, to have imposed "*their* forms" on Charlotte and the prince, so no one person can be said to be "guilty" of a breach of the forms. "Forms" is another key and shifting word in the book: people can "cheat each other with forms." Maggie thinks of "the funny form of our life" (as well she might), and there are dangerous moments of loss of con-fidence in forms. In fact, the new illicit symmetry is arrived at by a kind of group collusion and complicity.

But it doesn't end there. Maggie, who for the first part of the story seems all innocence and passive ignorance (not to say regres-sive childlikeness), becomes aware of the situation and begins to take action—quiet, quiet action—to bring about the restoration of the legitimate symmetries. Quiet—apart from the breaking of the bowl, about which a word. The "golden bowl" is the wedding present that Charlotte buys for the prince and Maggie. From the start, when they are buying it in the shop, there is much question as to whether it has a crack, or a flaw, or a split in it—concealed by the golden veneer. There is even a question as to whether it is real crystal or glass—and the further consideration that if you cannot see the crack, does it matter? ("But if it's something you can't find out, isn't it as good as if it were nothing?") And does real crystal split?

> "On lines and by laws of its own."
> "You mean if there's a weak place?"

In all this talk there is of course a clear double entendre; all that is said about the bowl is indirectly a questioning about marriage—or the two marriages in question, with their golden surfaces and concealed flaws and cracks and lines of potential breakage. It is not a symbol for us; it is one for the characters who use it as a way of talking about what would otherwise be unmentionable. When Maggie deliberately smashes the bowl, shattering it on the floor, it is clearly a way of saying that she now knows exactly what the relationship between Charlotte and the prince is, and how their marriages are all wrong and need to be reconstituted. She immediately starts to pick up the fragments (significantly, she can only pick up two at a time—adumbrating the final separation of the—effectively—ménage à quatre into proper couples). She announces her aspiration quite clearly: she wants "The golden bowl—as it *was* to have been. . . . The bowl with all happiness in it. The bowl without the crack." Her state of knowledge—and power—enables her to manipulate the prince and Charlotte, who increasingly do not know what Maggie knows, and therefore are increasingly her potential victims (and her father's). At the end, Maggie and the prince are back together again, while Adam is taking Charlotte back to America (always a less than desirable fate in James's fiction). Maggie maintains that she can bear anything and do anything "for love"; on one memorable occasion she repeats the phrase three times. And perhaps she does inaugurate a needed "new system" as she intends. The marriages hold. But questions remain.

We are reminded at the start of the machinery and the power ("the power of the rich peoples"), and Adam Verver for one (who is the source of the money, and thus the power and the machinery) is a very ambiguous figure. Adam is of course a favorite American name to suggest innocence, but James may well be offering a telling reappraisal of that oft-celebrated American innocence. Adam may be very ignorant or he may be very knowing—he is inscrutable (based, of course, on the American robber barons)—but he has all the power. His plan to build what he calls "American

City" back in America and fill it with all the precious objects he has acquired in Europe may have benevolent intentions, but it reveals a more dubious aspect of his collecting instinct, namely "his application of the same measure of value to such different pieces of property as old Persian carpets, say, and new human acquisitions." As Maggie tells the prince, he is "a part of his collection . . . a rarity, an object of beauty, an object of price." Treating or regarding people as things—even beautiful things—has never been an estimable practice in James. Adam's last cryptic comment as he looks at Maggie with her prince in their house is—"*Le compte y est.* You've got some good things." There is at least an undeniable suggestion in the book that if Maggie and Adam have "saved" the prince and Charlotte, they have also turned them into "human furniture." And when Adam leads Charlotte away it is, metaphorically, by "a long silken halter looped around her beautiful neck." The halter is invisible, of course, but we can see it and to see it is to see its cruelty. On one occasion when Maggie hears the trapped Charlotte taking some people round Adam's gallery she fancies that Charlotte's high voice sounds "like the shriek of a soul in pain."

Maggie is even more ambiguous. She can be described, metaphorically, variously as a doll, a slaughtered innocent, a resourceful settler, a divine saviour; there is, as it were, an excess of metaphor around her, putting her—and her actions—beyond any certain judgment. But one thing is clear: however passive she may be at the start, at the end she controls the action and realizes that the others are at her mercy—"There was no limit to her conceived design of not letting them escape." There is a note of something like glee in her realization that "they're paralysed, they're paralysed." "I make them do what I like," she all but boasts to Mrs. Assingham, and it is that inquiring onlooker who decided that "it will be Maggie herself who will mete out" all the punishments. By the end she sees the prince as being in "prison" and "caged" and once again it is with a thrill that she notes how he is "straitened and tied" by her superior manipulation of the situation. Maggie visits and comforts him in prison—the image is sustained—but then we have learned that her revenge was to be a subtle thing: it will consist of "compassionate patronage." Admittedly, all this is done "for love"—the motives and operations of which are fathomless enough. And there are those—many—who see Adam and Maggie as almost allegorical saviours and restorers of the crumbling relics and structures of European civilization, but that to me is too happy and facile a reading. There is too much awareness of the ambiguity of those forms which may be as ghastly as they are necessary (not to say funny); too much awareness that the new rearrangement rests on a felicitous deceit and a potentially ruthless power; too much sense of concealed evil, "the horror of the thing hideously *behind*, behind so much pretended, nobleness, cleverness, tenderness." In his Preface James refers to "the deeply involved and immersed and more or less bleeding participants," and while people in the book tend to use a concealingly hyperbolic vocabulary (everybody is "beautiful," "great," etc.), such words are surely bandages to hide the wounds or to negate the "horror of the thing hideously *behind*." This is not to say that James totally despaired of social structure and the maintaining form of marriage, nor of love—for there *is* love as well as passion (and revenge) in the book. He just knew what they could cost to be maintained. Just as he knew what the prince tells Maggie almost at the end of the book—"Everything's terrible, *cara*—in the heart of man."[1]

## VI

James finally published his reactions to America, after his return visit of 1904, in 1907 in *The American Scene*. It is an altogether remarkable book and it remains, as Edmund Wilson said, "one of the best books about modern America." It is interesting to note James's procedure in writing the book. Although he visited many friends and attended social functions, he cuts out almost entirely all reference to any dialogue with companions. This way he appears in the book as a "lone visionary," sending out his "lasso of observation," standing on the "verandahs of contemplation," a solitary "restless analyst" such as might have appeared in his own novels. His intercourse is with streets, buildings, vistas, and landscapes, all of which seem to address him with their murmured

---

1. Not that James was notably a democrat, but Alex de Tocqueville proved to be so prescient, even prophetic, about so many American phenomena that I cannot resist quoting him in this context when he asserts that "in democratic times what is most unstable, in the midst of the instability of everything, is the heart of man" (*Democracy in America*, 2. 4. 6).

apologies, their aggressive boasts, or their pathetic pleas, which he in turn answers. The most important dialogue is between Henry James and the American scene. One of the things that strikes him time and again is the seeming emptiness of America, an America visibly and audibly more crowded and busily pursuing "pecuniary gain" more avidly than ever before. "Void" and "vacancy" are perhaps the most frequent words in the book.

Before one judges this as a brand of patrician snobbery, it is instructive to try to discern the grounds for James's reaction to this new America of "florid creations waiting, a little bewilderingly, for their justification, waiting . . . for identity itself to come to them." He found a growing antipathy to recognizable distinctions and was struck by the strange homogenization of the emerging population—the way, for instance, an immigrant would lose the distinguishing qualities of his native identity without acquiring any new coloration from his new neighbors—"we surely fail to observe that the property washed out of the new subject begins to tint with its pink or azure his fellow-soakers in the terrible tank." This "terrible tank" is, of course, James's rephrasing of Walt Whitman's more optimistic image of America as a great "melting pot," and whether James is in Washington society or the New York Jewish ghetto, he is everywhere struck by the power of the "terrible tank" to dissolve distinctions, producing mass without meaning. The fluid emptiness that James recoiled from was at bottom a lack of forms communicating any sense of values, any deeply felt meaning—"it is as if the syllables were too numerous to make a legible word." For James the skyscraper (and New York struck him as like a "broken haircomb turned up") was the negation of significant form. "*They*, ranged in this terrible recent erection, were going to bring in money"—this, for James, was the featureless architecture of greed.

But as well as what Americans were putting up, it was what they were tearing down that distressed him: "What was taking place was a perpetual repudiation of the past." Seeking out the sites and buildings of his childhood, he found them all changed or obliterated. James's shock is not simply a conservative's preference for the old familiar forms. What worried him was that the new America did not seem to care enough for any of its new structures to wish to preserve them, "the very sign of its energy is that it doesn't believe in itself." A profound observation. It was America's "inability to convince . . . that she is serious about any form whatever, or about anything but that perpetual passionate pecuniary purpose which plays with all forms, which derides and devours them" that depressed James. The basic reasons he gives for the ugliness of the new America were "the so complete abolition of *forms*," and the production of new forms that were so "plastic," so "perpetually provisional."

Of course there are many fond evocations in the book and one can sense James's underlying love for the country. But where he detected ominous signs he recorded them. His observation, for instance, of "the way in which sane Society and pestilent City, in the United States, successfully cohabit" is followed by a "sense of a society dancing, all consciously, on the thin crust of a volcano"—a cluster of insights that have only gained in relevance. Or again, confronted by some young American women on a train, and the "innocently immodest ventilation of their puerile privacies," James has occasion to reconsider the position of the innocent American woman who had figured so richly in his fiction. He now imagines her making a silent plea to his "inward ear"— "Haven't I, however, as it is, been too abandoned and too *much* betrayed? Isn't it too late, and am I not, don't you think, practically lost?" Or again, the "haunting consciousness" of the Negro, which "is the prison of the Southern spirit," is elicited with extraordinary sensitivity.

If the scattered American syllables couldn't quite make up a word to say to James, James could listen and then try to formulate the appropriate speech. In his presence the American scene thus became, paradoxically, articulate in a unique way. And at the end James permits himself some very direct speaking to his compatriots: "You touch the great lonely land . . . only to plant upon it some ugliness about which, never dreaming of the grace of apology or contrition, you then proceed to brag with a cynicism all your own. . . . Is the germ of anything finely human, of anything agreeably or successfully social, supposedly planted in conditions of such endless stretching and such boundless spreading as shall appear finally to minister but to the triumph of the superficial and the apotheosis of the raw?" James speaks here with the license of an outraged or saddened close relation, but the deep relevance of his dialogue with the American scene is still as urgent as ever.

James's shorter fictions of this period pale somewhat beside his great novels, but they reveal, even crudely, just how bleak his late fictional world could be. Society is often less a matter for humor or idealization and more a jungle of "greedy wants, timid ideas and fishy passions" (as he wrote in *The Ivory Tower*). "Art is our flounderings shown," says one of his characters. Although the late short stories deal in the main with "small, smothered intensely private things," they often throw a thin, clear beam on human confusion and wounding. Characters flounder, and some of them drown in good earnest. Villains and victims tend to be more clearly discriminated: the former, addicted to "the sin of selfishness, the obsession of egotism," are often chilling and inhuman, while the latter—the failed and the forgotten, the robbed and the rejected, the appalled, the abused, the alienated—seem helplessly committed to a life of passive suffering and brooding (sometimes artistic) speculation. Instead of the fresh, open Daisy Miller, we now have the hard and socially ambitious "Miss Gunton of Poughkeepsie" and "the innocent egotism, the gilded and over-flowing anarchism" of the terrifyingly modern Mrs. Worthingham (in "Crapy Cornelia"). After that visit to America, James certainly had second thoughts about those bright young American women. Indeed, the muted but shocked asperity with which he portrays the unfeeling self-preoccupation of American society in "A Round of Visits" suggests that in some ways that return visit was traumatic. "The Jolly Corner" concerns the return of an expatriate to America, where he has to face—in ghost form—the alter ego of what he might have been if he had stayed in America. Far from being a pleasant or curious experience, it results in all but fatal nightmare.

The victims in the late tales seem to be almost shocked or stupefied into immobility and silence. A typical figure is an aging man sitting down in sorrow and solitude, abandoning himself to melancholy musing and waiting for the deepening twilight to close in. He may feel estranged, excluded, unwanted and unfulfilled; life, somehow, has eluded his too tentative grasp—or his too fastidious egoism (as in "The Bench of Desolation"). For consolation these figures have a developed consciousness. "He could now stare but at the prospect of exclusion, and of his walking round it, through the coming years"—that is the self-effacing figure of Traffle in "Mora Montravers." As the night comes on he has, for company, his private almost Jamesian mind and imagination—"exquisite, occult, dangerous and sacred, to which everything ministered and which nothing could take away." Many of these late Jamesian protagonists opt for renunciation because the cruel stridency and harsh untempered friction of modern life is simply too much for them (they prefer "The Tone of Time")—or, more subtly, it is intimated that their renunciation may be traced to a dangerous, solipsistic overestimation of the self. So it is in the great story "The Beast in the Jungle" mentioned above, in which James explored to the full the subtle horror that could lie in this commitment to a life of renunciation. John Marcher, convinced a special destiny awaits him, is too aridly self-enwrapped to recognize the chance for a full human relationship that May Bartram presents to him. She loves him; he loves himself too much to perceive the fact, or indeed even to see "the other" at all. She dies, and he feels no special grief. Then he sees someone in the graveyard, someone genuinely grief-stricken. The terrible truth starts to dawn: "no passion had ever touched him, for this was what passion meant; he had survived and maundered and pined, but where had been *his* deep ravage?" The moment of truth—it is the leap of the beast—is blindingly simple and terrible: "he had been the man of his time, *the* man, to whom nothing on earth was to have happened." This story, above all, is the one to remember when reading the great novels of this period.

James left two unfinished novels at his death. *The Ivory Tower* was started in 1913, but abandoned when the advent of war made it seem impossible to continue—nevertheless, there is enough of it to allow us to see its continuity with the previous novels. Again it concerns passions and possessions, exploitations and renunciations, and, above all, money. The book opens with scenes concerning two dying millionaires. One, rather obviously named Betterman, is lingering on to see a distant relative, a young American innocent who has been brought up in Europe (Graham Fielder), who is returning to see him. It is made clear that Betterman, having satisfied himself that Fielder is absolutely untainted by the business world, having had no contact with the "awful game of grab" which seems to dominate American society, will leave him all his money. It is made equally clear that Fielder will find a way of relinquishing that money to a mercenary and predatory "friend." Dominant is a sense of an America obsessed with the "money-passion," the spirit of "ferocious acquisition." Society is "all senseless sound and expensive futility." It is at once still "innocent" and "unspeakably corrupt"; it is, in the words of James's notes, "the dreadful American money-world." Graham Fielder is to gain a vivid impression of "so many of the black and merciless things that are behind the great possessions." And since he is, rather like Strether, by nature "an out and out non-producer" and "non-accumulator," he will find a way of disassociating himself from his inheritance—getting out of the game (the symbol of the "ivory tower" is used in this context). He will be another Jamesian observer-appreciator: "He really enjoys getting so detached from it as to be able to have it before him for observation and wonder as he does. . . ." Among other things, the novel would have been a quite savage indictment of an America in which James felt a man of his kind of consciousness and sensibility could no longer live—a rejection of his own American heritage.

*The Sense of the Past* seems to have been started in 1900 and taken up again briefly in 1906. It was the novel James was working on when he died. In an odd way it seems to project a latent horror of the European past, as *The Ivory Tower* revealed a very manifest horror of the American present. The novel has a perfect—and familiar—subject for James. It concerns yet another of his passionate pilgrims for whom Europe is an experience, ambivalent to the point of annihilation. Ralph Pendrel is a young American who has never visited Europe but has somehow developed a highly refined and appreciative "sense of the past." He inherits a Georgian house from a remote relative in England and goes to take possession. So animated are his susceptibilities and expectations that when he finally does enter the house he "disappears into the Past." He walks into a family situation of 1820 in which he is the expected American relation. At first the adventure is exhilarating. He finds he can successfully play and improvise the role expected of him, and he enjoys this seemingly actual immersion in a past he had hitherto only dreamed of. But the adventure starts to turn dark—moments of rapture give place to sudden chills and fears as he realizes that his 1820 relatives are beginning to find him somehow strange. James intended to stress "the slow growth on the part of the others of their fear of Ralph, even in the midst of their making much of him, as abnormal, as uncanny, as not *like* those they know of their own kind etc., etc.; and his fear just *of* theirs, with his double consciousness, alas, of his being *almost* as right as possible for the 'period,' and yet so intimately and secretly wrong." Through maneuvers of plot it was intended that he should finally be saved: "saved from all the horror of the growing fear of *not* being saved, of being lost, of being *in* in the past to stay, heart-breakingly to stay and never know his own original precious Present again." His dread—James intended to emphasize it—was of his being "never saved, never rescued, never restored again, by the termination of his adventure and his experience, to his native temporal conditions, which he yearns for with an unutterable yearning. He has come to have his actual ones, the benighted, the dreadful ones, in horror. . . ." However James would have resolved the novel, we can note a deep ambivalence which is perhaps symptomatic of his whole work (and life?). Ralph longs for the past, but when it threatens to imprison him, he yearns for "his own original precious Present," "his native temporal conditions." And yet what that present, what those conditions were like, James had portrayed in *The Ivory Tower*. Truly, where—actually and imaginatively—was one to live? And where, anymore, for someone like James, could there be a "home"? Clearly, one answer could only be "in writing."

James's other major work during his last period was what has come to be called *The Autobiographies*, which consists of *A Small Boy and Others* (1913), *Notes of a Son and Brother* (1914), and *The Middle Years*, left uncompleted at his death. Although initially intended to be an account of his family, in particular of his brother William, James confines himself almost entirely to the history and development of his own consciousness—its confusions and gratitudes, its bewilderments and wonders, its experience of the strangeness of life, and its intimations of the grace of art. Here are some of the ways in which he refers to his relationship to the past: "Remembrance steals on me. . . . I woo it all back. . . . I turn round again to where I left myself gasping. . . . Let me hurry, however, to catch again that thread. . . . I scarce know why, nor do I much, I confess, distinguish occasions—but I see what I see. . . . I lose myself under the whole pressure of the spring of memory. . . . I meet another acute unguarded reminiscence. . . ." James apologizes for leaving "the straighter line of my narrative." He "gleans" memories from things, "not minding that later dates are involved." He is totally indifferent to external chronology, the unilinear history of physical events: he has a rarely subtle sense of the mysterious commerce between present consciousness and those past states of consciousness preserved in the intermittent brilliances of memory. He uses words like "surrendering" and "succumbing" to the past; thus, "I live back of a sudden—for I insist on just yielding to it." It is rather as if James's mind was wandering through the museum of his own memory, responding to sudden gleams and forgotten echoes, alternatively wooing and yielding to the still-vibrant impressions that are stored in the recesses of his consciousness:

> I foresee moreover how little I shall be able to resist, through these Notes, the force of persuasion expressed in the individual *vivid* image of the past wherever encountered, these images having always such terms of their own, such subtle secrets and insidious arts for keeping us in relation with them, for bribing us by the beauty, the authority, the wonder of their saved intensity. They have saved it, they seem to say to us, from such a welter of death and darkness and ruin that this alone makes a value and a light and a dignity for them, something indeed of an argument that our story, since we attempt to tell one, has lapses and gaps without them.

The story *is*, indeed, the sequence of preserved images that furnished James's own consciousness. In actual life, all tends to death and darkness and ruin. The past, in reality, is so much "imponderable dust." The human consciousness, as long as it is still conscious, performs a great act of salvage and rescue, simply by remembering, recalling the stored-up images. The human consciousness saves what life merely wastes.

James loves to evoke what he calls the "tiny particles of history"; that is why he will spend pages recapturing a room, someone's clothes, a facial appearance, a sudden tremor of delight or fear; as he beautifully puts it, "the passion, that may reside in a single pulse of time." But his subject was centrally himself. He describes it in this way: "the personal history as it were, of an imagination, a lively one of course . . . had always struck me as a task that a teller of tales might rejoice in, his advance through it conceivably causing at each step some rich precipitation." Whom should he choose? "He had been with me all the while and only too obscurely and intimately. . . . I had in a word to draw him forth from within rather than meet him in the world before me, the more convenient sphere of the objective, and to make him objective, in short had to turn nothing less than myself inside out." So, in his autobiographies, James is turning his consciousness inside out, trying to recapture what went into it to turn it into the consciousness of a novelist, an artist. He writes in a twilight mood, but far from despair; a mood in which meditation, comprehension, and compassion are at one:

> the beauty of the main truth as to any remembered matter
> looked at in due detachment, or in other words through the
> haze of time, is that comprehension has then become one with
> criticism, compassion, as it may really be called, one with
> musing vision, and the whole company of the anciently restless,
> with their elations and mistakes, their sincerities and fallacies
> and vanities and triumphs, embalmed for us in the mild essence
> of their collective submission to fate.

The past was imponderable dust; and the present (the First World War) was dark indeed, and James does not at all slight or mitigate the darkness, death, and ruin in life. But over against it he continued to hold up "the wonder of 'consciousness.' It is, in the deepest sense, an 'act of life.' "

James sent a copy of *Notes of a Son and Brother* to his friend Henry Adams—whose response seems to have been one of extreme pessimism and melancholy. We do not have his letter to James, but we have James's marvelous reply, which includes these words, incomparably poised in their tone:

> My dear Henry,
>               I have your melancholy outpouring of the 7th,
> and I know not how better to acknowledge it than by the full
> recognition of its unmitigated blackness. *Of course* we are lone
> survivors, of course the past that was our lives is at the bottom
> of the abyss—if the abyss *has* any bottom; of course, too,
> there's no use talking unless one particularly *wants* to. But the
> purpose, almost, of my printed divagations was to show that
> one *can*, strange to say, still want to—or at least can behave as
> if one did. Behold me therefore so behaving—and apparently
> capable of continuing to do so. I still find my consciousness
> interesting—under *cultivation* of the interest. . . . *Why* mine

yields an interest I don't know that I can tell you, but I don't challenge or quarrel with it—I encourage it with a ghastly grin. You see I still, in the presence of life (or of what you deny to be such) have reactions—as many as possible—and the book I sent you is a proof of them. It's, I suppose, because I am that queer monster, the artist, an obstinate finality, an inexhaustible sensibility. Hence the reactions—appearances, memories, many things, go on playing upon it with consequences that I note and "enjoy" (grim word!) noting. It all takes doing—and I *do*. I believe I shall do it again—it is still an act of life.

It would be hard to find a more eloquent justification—or apologia—for that queer monster, that obstinate finality—the artist.

## VII

In conclusion, here are two quotations which speak for themselves, for James, for the whole mystery—and indispensability—of James's unique kind of attitude and art. The first is from a letter to Grace Norton—that most difficult kind of letter to write, one of consolation to someone recently bereaved. James speaks of the "gift of life" to one mourning in the shadow of death.

Life is the most valuable thing we know anything about, and it is therefore a great mistake to surrender it while there is any yet left in the cup. In other words consciousness is an illimitable power, and though at times it may seem to be all consciousness of misery, yet in the way it propagates itself from wave to wave, so that we never cease to feel, and though at moments we appear to, try to, pray to, there is something that holds one in one's place, makes it a standpoint in the universe which it is probably good not to forsake.

And the other quotation is from his notebooks of 1905 after he has visited the family cemetery.

Everything was there, everything *came*; the recognition, stillness, the strangeness, the pity and the sanctity and the terror, the breath-catching passion and the divine relief of tears. William's inspired transcript, on the exquisite little Florentine urn of Alice's ashes, William's divine gift to us, and to *her*, of the Dantean lines—

Dopo lungo esilio e martirio
Viene a questa pace—

took me so by the throat by its penetrating *rightness*, that it was as if one sank down on one's knees in a kind of anguish of gratitude before something for which one had waited with a long, deep *ache*. But why do I write of the all unutterable and the all abysmal? Why does my pen not drop from my hand on approaching the infinite pity and tragedy of all the past? It does, poor helpless pen, with what it meets of the ineffable, what it meets of the cold Medusa-face of life, of all the life *lived*, on every side. *Basta, basta*!

# A Select Bibliography

## BIBLIOGRAPHY

*A Bibliography of the Writings of Henry James.* Le Roy Phillips. 1906;
   new edition, 1930.
*A Bibliography of Henry James.* Leon Edel and D. H. Laurence. 1957;
   3d revised edition, 1982.


## COLLECTED WORKS

*Collected Novels and Tales.* 14 vols. 1883.
*The Novels and Tales.* 26 vols. 1907–1909. With special prefaces and
   textual revisions for volumes 1–24.
*Uniform Edition of the Tales.* 14 vols. 1915–1919.
*Novels and Stories.* Edited by P. Lubbock. 35 vols. 1921–1923.
*The American Novels and Stories.* 1947.
*The Scenic Art.* Edited by A. Wade. 1948. Collected papers on the theater.
*The Complete Plays.* Edited by Leon Edel. 1949.
*The American Essays.* Edited by Leon Edel. 1956.
*Literary Reviews and Essays.* Edited by A. Mordell. 1957.
*The Complete Tales.* Edited by Leon Edel. 12 vols. 1962–1964.
*The Novels.* Introduction by Leon Edel. 1967–.
*The Collected Literary Criticism.* 2 vols. Edited by Leon Edel. 1984.


## SELECTED WORKS

*Fourteen Stories.* Edited by D. Garnett. 1946.
*Ten Short Stories.* Edited by M. Swan. 1948.
*The House of Fiction: Essays on the Novel.* Edited by Leon Edel. 1957.
*Selected Letters.* Edited by Leon Edel. 1956.
*Selected Stories.* Edited by A. Hopkins. 1957. In the World's Classics
   Edition.
*Selected Literary Criticism.* Edited by M. Shapira. 1963.

*Stories of the Supernatural.* Edited by Leon Edel. 1971.
*The Tales of Henry James.* Edited by M. Aziz. Vol. 1, 1973.

### SEPARATE WORKS

*A Passionate Pilgrim and Other Tales.* 1875. Stories.
*Transatlantic Sketches.* 1875. Travel.
*Roderick Hudson.* 1876 (1875). Novel.
*The American.* 1877. Novel.
*French Poets and Novelists.* 1878. Criticism.
*Watch and Ward.* 1878. Novel.
*The Europeans.* 2 vols. 1878. Novel.
*Daisy Miller.* 2 vols. 1879 (1878). Stories.
*The Madonna of the Future and Other Tales.* 2 vols. 1879. Stories.
*Confidence.* 2 vols. 1880 (1879). Novel.
*Hawthorne.* 1879. Criticism.
*The Diary of a Man of Fifty* and *A Bundle of Letters.* 1880. Stories.
*Washington Square.* 2 vols. 1881 (1880). Stories.
*The Portrait of a Lady.* 3 vols. 1881. Novel.
*The Siege of London.* 1883. Stories.
*Portraits of Places.* 1883. Travel.
*A Little Tour in France.* 1885 (1884). Travel.
*Tales of Three Cities.* 1884. Stories.
*Stories Revived.* 3 vols. 1885. Stories.
*The Bostonians.* 3 vols. 1886. Novel.
*The Princess Casamassima.* 3 vols. 1886. Novel.
*Partial Portraits.* 1888. Criticism.
*The Reverberator.* 2 vols. 1888. Novel.
*The Aspern Papers.* 2 vols. 1888. Stories.
*A London Life.* 2 vols. 1889. Stories.
*The Tragic Muse.* 2 vols. 1890. Novel.
*The Lesson of the Master.* 1892. Stories.
*The Real Thing and Other Tales.* 1893. Stories.
*Picture and Text.* 1893. Criticism.
*The Private Life.* 1893. Stories.
*Essays in London and Elsewhere.* 1893. Criticism.
*Theatricals.* 1894. Plays.
*Theatricals: Second Series.* 1895. Plays.
*Terminations.* 1895. Stories.
*Embarrassments.* 1896. Stories.
*The Other House.* 2 vols. 1896. Novel.
*The Spoils of Poynton.* 1897. Novel.
*What Maisie Knew.* 1897. Novel.
*In the Cage.* 1898. Story.

*The Two Magics.* 1898. Stories.
*The Awkward Age.* 1899. Novel.
*The Soft Side.* 1900. Stories.
*The Sacred Fount.* 1901. Novel.
*The Wings of the Dove.* 2 vols. 1902. Novel.
*The Better Sort.* 1903. Stories.
*The Ambassadors.* 1903. Novel.
*William Wetmore Story and His Friends.* 2 vols. 1903. Biography.
*The Golden Bowl.* 2 vols. 1904. Novel.
*The Question of Our Speech* and *The Lesson of Balzac.* 1905. Two lectures; criticism.
*English Hours.* 1905. Travel.
*The American Scene.* 1907. Travel.
*Views and Reviews.* 1908. Criticism.
*Julia Bride.* 1909. Story.
*Italian Hours.* 1909. Travel.
*The Finer Grain.* 1910. Stories.
*The Outcry.* 1911. Novel.
*A Small Boy and Others.* 1913. Autobiography.
*Notes of a Son and Brother.* 1914. Autobiography.
*Notes on Novelists.* 1914. Criticism.
*The Ivory Tower.* 1917. Unfinished novel.
*The Sense of the Past.* 1917. Unfinished novel.
*The Middle Years.* 1917. Autobiography.
*Gabrielle de Bergerac.* 1918. Story.
*Within the Rim and Other Essays.* 1919. Essays.
*Travelling Companions.* 1919. Stories.
*Notes and Reviews.* 1921. Criticism.
*The Art of the Novel: Critical Prefaces.* Edited by R. P. Blackmur. 1934.
*The Notebooks of Henry James.* Edited by F. O. Matthiessen and K. B. Murdock. 1947.
*The Art of Fiction and Other Essays.* Edited by M. Roberts. 1948.
*Eight Uncollected Tales.* 1950.
*The Painter's Eye: Notes and Essays on the Pictorial Arts.* Edited by J. L. Sweeney. 1956.
*Parisian Sketches, 1875–76.* Edited by Leon Edel and I. D. Lind. 1957.

## LETTERS

*The Letters of Henry James.* Selected and edited by P. Lubbock. 2 vols. 1920.
*Letters of Henry James to Walter Berry.* 1928.
*Theatre and Friendship: Some Henry James Letters.* Edited by E. Robins. 1932.

*Henry James and H. G. Wells: A Record of Their Friendship, Their Debate on the Art of Fiction, and Their Quarrel.* Edited with an introduction by Leon Edel and G. N. Ray. 1958.

*Switzerland in the Life and Work of Henry James.* 1966. Includes hitherto unpublished letters of James to Mrs. Clara Benedict.

*Letters of Henry James.* Edited by Leon Edel. 4 vols. 1975–1984.


SOME CRITICAL AND BIOGRAPHICAL STUDIES

*The Novels of Henry James.* Elizabeth Cary. 1905. The first critical book on James's work.

*Henry James.* Rebecca West. 1916.

*Henry James: A Critical Study.* F. M. Hueffer. 1913.

*The Method of Henry James.* J. W. Beach. 1918.

*Instigations.* E. Pound. 1920. Contains an essay on James.

*The Craft of Fiction.* P. Lubbock. 1921. There are constant references to James throughout this work.

*Notes on Life and Letters.* J. Conrad. 1921. Contains an appreciation of James.

*Readers and Writers.* A. R. Orage. 1922. Contains an essay on James.

*Henry James at Work.* Theodora Bosanquet. 1924. A portrait by James's secretary.

*The Pilgrimage of Henry James.* Van Wyck Brooks. 1925. A study of James as an expatriate novelist.

*Theory and Practice in Henry James.* Herbert L. Hughes. 1925.

*Henry James: Man and Author.* Pelham Edgar. 1927.

*The Sense of Glory.* H. Read. 1929. Contains an essay on James.

*Early Developments of Henry James.* Cornelia P. Kelley. 1930.

*Les Années Dramatiques.* Leon Edel. 1931.

*The Prefaces of Henry James.* Leon Edel. 1931.

*Portraits.* D. MacCarthy. 1931. Contains a portrait of James.

*The Three Jameses: A Family of Minds.* C. Hartley Grattan. 1932.

*A Backward Glance.* Edith Wharton. 1934. Mrs. Wharton's autobiography, containing many references to James.

*The Georgian Literary Scene.* F. A. Swinnerton. 1935. Contains an essay on James.

*The Thought and Character of Henry James.* R. B. Perry. 2 vols. 1935.

*The Modern Fables of Henry James.* Edwin M. Snell. 1935.

*The Destructive Element.* Stephen Spender. 1935. Contains essays on James.

*The Triple Thinkers.* Edmund Wilson. 1938. Contains the essay "The Ambiguity of Henry James."

*Henry James: The Major Phase*. F. O. Matthiessen. 1944.

*The Legend of the Master*. Edited by S. Nowell Smith. 1947. An anthology of reminiscences of James.

*The Question of Henry James*. Edited by F. W. Dupee. 1945.

*The James Family: A Group Biography*. F. O. Matthiessen. 1947.

*Henry James and the Expanding Horizon*. Osborn Andreas. 1948.

*The Great Tradition*. F. R. Leavis. 1949.

*The Crooked Corridor: A Story of Henry James*. Elizabeth Stevenson. 1949.

*Henry James*. F. W. Dupee. 1951.

*Les Lettres Américaines devant la Critique Française (1887–1917)*. C. Arnavon. 1952.

*The Common Pursuit*. F. R. Leavis. 1952.

*Henry James*. Leon Edel. Vol. 1: *The Untried Years, 1843–69*, 1953; vol. 2: *The Conquest of London, 1870–83*, 1962; vol. 3: *The Middle Years, 1884–94*, 1963; vol. 4: *The Treacherous Years: 1895–1901*, 1969; vol. 5: *The Master, 1901–1916*, 1972.

*Young Henry James: 1843–1870*. R. C. LeClair. 1955.

*The Themes of Henry James*. E. T. Bowden. 1956.

*The American Henry James*. Q. Anderson. 1958.

*The American Novel and Its Tradition*. R. Chase. 1958.

*Henry James*. D. W. Jefferson. 1960. In the Writers and Critics Series.

*James's Later Novels*. R. Marks. 1960.

*The Comic Sense of Henry James: A Study of the Early Novels*. W. R. Poirier. 1960.

*A Casebook on Henry James's "Turn of the Screw."* Edited by G. Willen. 1960.

*The Houses That James Built and Other Literary Studies*. R. W. Stallman. 1961.

*The Novels of Henry James*. O. Cargill. 1961.

*The Ordeal of Consciousness in Henry James*. Dorothea Krook. 1962.

*Henry James and His Cult*. Maxwell Geismar. 1964.

*The Expense of Vision: Essays on the Craft of Henry James*. Laurence Holland. 1964.

*Henry James and the Modern Reader*. D. W. Jefferson. 1964.

*The Battle and the Books: Some Aspects of Henry James*. Edward Stone. 1964.

*Plots and Characters in the Novels of Henry James*. R. Gale. 1964.

*The Imagination of Loving*. Naomi Lebowitz. 1965.

*Edith Wharton and Henry James: The Story of Their Friendship*. Millicent Bell. 1965.

*Henry James: A Reader's Guide*. Samuel G. Putt. 1966. Reprinted in paperback as *The Fiction of Henry James*.

*Perspectives on James's "The Portrait of a Lady."* Edited by William T. Stafford. 1967.

*The Search for Form: Studies in the Structure of James's Fiction.* J. A. Ward. 1967.

*Henry James.* Edited by R. Gard. 1968. The Critical Heritage Series.

*Henry James.* Edited by Tony Tanner. 1968. Modern Judgments Series.

*Strange Alloy—The Relation of Tragedy and Comedy in the Fiction of Henry James.* E. D. Leyburn. 1968.

*The Negative Imagination: Form and Perspective in the Novels of Henry James.* S. Sears. 1968.

*Henry James at Home.* H. Montgomery Hyde. 1969.

*The Early Tales of Henry James.* J. Kraft. 1969.

*The Grasping Imagination: The American Writings of Henry James.* P. Buitenhuis. 1970.

*Twentieth Century Interpretations of "The Turn of the Screw" and Other Tales.* Edited by J. Tompkins. 1970.

*The Ambiguity of Henry James.* C. T. Samuels. 1971.

*Henry James and the Requirements of the Imagination.* Philip M. Weinstein. 1971.

*"Air of Reality": New Essays on Henry James.* Edited by J. Goode. 1972.

*Henry James: The Ibsen Years.* Michael Egan. 1972.

*"Sensuous Pessimism": Italy in the Work of Henry James.* Carl Maves. 1973.

*Henry James and His World.* H. T. Moore. 1974. A pictorial biography.

*Henry James: The Drama of Fulfilment, An Approach to the Novels.* Kenneth Graham. 1975.

*Henry James: The Creative Process.* Harold T. McCarthy. 1975.

*Henry James: The Lessons of the Master: Popular Fiction and Personal Style in the Nineteenth Century.* W. Veeder. 1975.

*Who's Who in Henry James.* Edited by Glenda Leeming. 1976.

*Communities of Honor and Love in Henry James.* M. MacKenzie. 1976.

*Henry James and Henry Adams: The Emergence of a Modern Consciousness.* John C. Rowe. 1976.

*Language and Knowledge in the Late Novels of Henry James.* Ruth B. Yeazell. 1976.

*The Melodramatic Imagination: Balzac, Henry James, Melodrama and the Mode of Excess.* P. Brooks. 1976.

*The Fiction of Henry James: Plots and Characters.* Robert Gale. 1977.

*The Concept of Ambiguity: The Example of Henry James.* Shlomith Rimmon. 1977.

*Eve and Henry James: Portraits of Women and Girls in His Fiction.* Edward Wagenknecht. 1978.

*Henry James and the Experimental Novel.* S. Perosa. 1978.

*Nietzsche, Henry James, and the Artistic Will.* Stephen Donadio. 1978.
*The Novels of Henry James: A Study of Culture and Consciousness.* Brian
    Lee. 1978.
*A Rhetoric of Literary Character: Some Women of Henry James.* Mary
    D. Springer. 1978.
*Tragedy in the Victorian Novel: Theory and Practice in the Novels of
    George Eliot, Thomas Hardy and Henry James.* Jeanette King. 1978.
*Henry James: A Reference Guide, 1917–1959.* Edited by K. P. McCol-
    gan. 1979.
*Henry James: A Reference Guide, 1960–1974.* Edited by D. Scura. 1979.
*Henry James and Flaubert: A Study of Contrasts.* D. Gervais. 1979.
*Henry James and Germany.* Evelyn A. Hovanec. 1979.
*The Later Novels of Henry James.* Nicola Bradbury. 1979.
*Writing and Reading in Henry James.* Susanne Kappeler. 1980.
*Culture and Conduct in the Novels of Henry James.* A. Berland. 1981.
*The Uses of Obscurity: The Fiction of Early Modernism.* Allon White.
    1981. One-third of the book is on James.
*Diary of Alice James.* Edited with an introduction by Leon Edel. 1982.
*The Insecure World of Henry James's Fiction: Intensity and Ambiguity.*
    Ralf Norrman. 1982.
*Balzac, James and the Realistic Novel.* W. Stowe. 1983.

### INDEX OF SHORT STORIES

*The title in italics refers to the volume in which the story appears.*

Covering End, *The Two Magics*
Coxon Fund, The, *Terminations*
Crapy Cornelia, *The Finer Grain*
Crawford's Consistency, *Eight Uncollected Tales*
Daisy Miller, *Daisy Miller*
Day of Days, A, *Stories Revived*
Death of the Lion, The, *Terminations*
De Grey: A Romance, *Travelling Companions*
Diary of a Man of Fifty, The, *The Madonna of the Future and Other Tales*
Eugene Pickering, *A Passionate Pilgrim*
"Europe," *The Soft Side*
Faces, The [as The Two Faces], *The Better Sort*
Figure in the Carpet, The, *Embarrassments*
Flickerbridge, *The Better Sort*
Fordham Castle, *Novels and Tales,* New York edition, vol. 16
Four Meetings, *Daisy Miller*
Friends of the Friends, The [as The Way It Came], *Embarrassments*
Gabrielle de Bergerac, *Gabrielle de Bergerac*
Georgina's Reasons, *Stories Revived*
Ghostly Rental, The, *Ghostly Tales*
Given Case, The, *The Soft Side*
Glasses, *Embarrassments*
Great Condition, The, *The Soft Side*
Great Good Place, The, *The Soft Side*
Greville Fane, *The Real Thing and Other Tales*
Guest's Confession, *Travelling Companions*
Impressions of a Cousin, The, *Tales of Three Cities*
International Episode, An, *Daisy Miller*
In the Cage, *In the Cage*
Jersey Villas [as Sir Dominick Ferrand], *The Real Thing and Other Tales*
John Delavoy, *The Soft Side*
Jolly Corner, The, *Novels and Tales,* New York edition, vol. 17
Julia Bride, *Julia Bride*
Lady Barberina, *Tales of Three Cities*
Landscape Painter, A, *Stories Revived*
Last of the Valerii, The, *A Passionate Pilgrim and Other Tales*
Lesson of the Master, The, *The Lesson of the Master*
Liar, The, *A London Life*
Light Man, A, *Stories Revived*
London Life, A, *A London Life*
Longstaff's Marriage, *The Madonna of the Future and Other Tales*
Lord Beaupre, *The Private Life and Other Tales*
Louisa Pallant, *The Aspern Papers*

Madame De Mauves, *A Passionate Pilgrim and Other Tales*
Marriages, The, *The Lesson of the Master*
Master Eustace, *Stories Revived*
Maud-Evelyn, *The Soft Side*
Middle Years, The, *Termination*
Miss Gunton of Poughkeepsie, *The Soft Side*
Modern Warning, The, *The Aspern Papers*
Mora Montravers, *The Finer Grain*
Most Extraordinary Case, A, *Stories Revived*
Mrs. Medwin, *The Better Sort*
Mrs. Temperley, *A London Life*
My Friend Bingham, *Eight Uncollected Tales*
Nest Time, The, *Embarrassments*
New England Winter, A, *Tales of Three Cities*
Nona Vincent, *The Real Thing and Other Tales*
Osborne's Revenge, *Eight Uncollected Tales*
Owen Wingrave, *The Private Life*
Pandora, *Stories Revived*
Papers, The, *The Better Sort*
Passionate Pilgrim, A, *A Passionate Pilgrim and Other Tales*
Paste, *The Soft Side*
Patagonia, The, *A London Life*
Path of Duty, The, *Stories Revived*
Pension Beaurepas, The, *Washington Square*
Point of View, The, *The Siege of London*
Poor Richard, *Stories Revived*
Private Life, The, *The Private Life*
Problem, A, *Eight Uncollected Tales*
Professor Fargo, *Travelling Companions*
Pupil, The, *The Lesson of the Master*
Real Right Thing, The, *The Soft Side*
Romance of Certain Old Clothes, The, *A Passionate Pilgrim and Other Tales*
Rose-Agathe, *Stories Revived*
Round of Visits, A, *The Finer Grain*
Siege of London, The, *The Siege of London*
Sir Dominick Ferrand, *The Real Thing and Other Tales*
Sir Edmund Orme, *The Lesson of the Master*
Solution, The, *The Lesson of the Master*
Special Type, The, *The Better Sort*
Story in It, The, *The Better Sort*
Story of a Masterpiece, The, *Eight Uncollected Tales*
Story of a Year, The, *American Novels and Stories*

Sweetheart of M. Brisieux, The, *Travelling Companions*
Theodolinde, *Stories Revived*
Third Person, The, *The Soft Side*
Tone of Time, The, *The Better Sort*
Travelling Companions, *Travelling Companions*
Tree of Knowledge, The, *The Soft Side*
Turn of the Screw, The, *The Two Magics*
Two Countries [as The Modern Warning], *The Aspern Papers*
Two Faces, The, *The Better Sort*
Two Magics, The, *The Two Magics*
Velvet Glove, The, *The Finer Grain*
Visits, The, *The Private Life*
Way It Came, The, *Embarrassments*
Wheel of Time, The, *The Private Life*